Helen Philipps'
CROSS STITCH
SAMPLERS AND CARDS

Over 55 designs from the heart

David & Charles

To Sarah and Rosie
with all my love.

If daughters were flowers
you're the ones I'd pick.

A DAVID & CHARLES BOOK

First published in the UK in 2004
Designs, text and decorative artwork Copyright © Helen Philipps 2004
Photography and layout Copyright © David & Charles 2004

Distributed in North America
by F&W Publications, Inc.
4700 East Galbraith Road
Cincinnati, OH 45236
1-800-289-0963

A catalogue record for this book is available from the British Library.
ISBN 0 7153 1582 X

Executive commissioning editor Cheryl Brown
Desk editor Ame Verso
Executive art editor Ali Myer
Art editor Prudence Rogers
Project editor and chart preparation Lin Clements
Photography Simon Whitmore

Printed in Singapore by KHL Printing Co Pte Ltd
for David & Charles
Brunel House   Newton Abbot   Devon

Visit our website at www.davidandcharles.co.uk

David & Charles books are available from all good bookshops; alternatively you can contact
our Orderline on (0)1626 334555 or write to us at FREEPOST EX2110, David & Charles Direct,
Newton Abbot TQ12 4ZZ (no stamp required UK mainland).

Contents

Introduction

This book is filled with designs for family and friends, to stitch from the heart with love and affection. You will find a wealth of modern, fresh sampler and card designs, with strong images and pretty colours.

The designs are grouped into seasonal chapters, beginning with a new home sampler in Spring and moving through the year to the festive images of Christmas. Each season concludes with a selection of cards, ideal quick-stitch projects for when time is short. Additional alphabets and messages have also been provided on pages 100–102 so you can personalize the samplers and even design your own cards and keepsakes.

In the past, samplers often incorporated a moral verse into their design to help inspire the young girls who were sewing them. Today, we frequently stitch a sampler as an expression of affection for someone or to help us feel positive. The moral verses have become loving messages or motivational and inspirational sayings. Some sampler phrases and quotations from the past are still in use today, for example, the timeless 'home sweet home' was often found in Victorian homes but which is still enjoyed by many and has a place in this book.

Samplers that celebrate special events are always popular as they make wonderful keepsakes. A wedding, the birth of a new baby and golden and silver wedding anniversaries are all occasions that are perfect to stitch for, and all have a sampler in this book. There are also samplers especially for celebrating friendship, like the bright bulb-filled Friendship in Bloom.

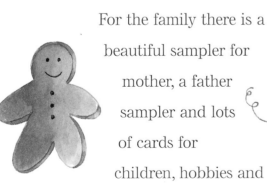

For the family there is a beautiful sampler for mother, a father sampler and lots of cards for children, hobbies and celebrations of all kinds.

The Winter section begins with an advent calendar, followed by a fun gingerbread men design, sweet angels perfect to give to friends as gifts and many lovely Christmas cards. As the year turns full circle there is a sampler for New Year inspired by an Irish blessing, to bring good wishes for the future.

I hope there is something for everyone in the many designs included in this book and that you will have fun stitching them, either for yourself or to make up into gifts for friends and family. Enjoy the delights of the seasons in your stitching.

Spring

Everyone looks forward to spring and the many joys it brings, like warm sunshine, bulbs, birds and blossom. This section of the book brings all those things: you'll find samplers for a new home, a new baby, a beautiful floral sampler for mother's day and a bright friendship sampler. There is also a charming selection of greetings cards, including some for a new home, Easter and birthdays.

New Home Sampler

If you know someone moving house why not stitch this fresh and pretty sampler for them?
This design celebrates a new home, with bright morning glories and colourful birdhouses surrounding
an idyllic country cottage. The sampler can be stitched on linen or Aida.

28 x 23cm (11 x 9in) antique
white 28-count linen
or 14-count Aida

DMC stranded cotton (floss)
as in the chart key

Size 26 tapestry needle

Stitch count 100 x 78
Design size 18 x 14cm (7⅛ x 5½in)

1 Bind the edges of the fabric or oversew to prevent fraying. Fold the fabric in half, then in half again to find the centre and begin stitching from the centre of the chart overleaf.

2 Use two strands of stranded cotton (floss) for cross stitches and three-quarter cross stitches. Use one strand for the backstitching and outlining, except for the plant stems and tendrils which use two strands. Stitch over two threads of linen or one block of Aida.

3 When all the stitching is complete, press your work carefully and frame as a picture (see page 98 for advice).

Ideas
The little pink cottage would make a lovely greetings card, and the birds and birdhouses could be stitched on to Aida band and used to decorate kitchen accessories.

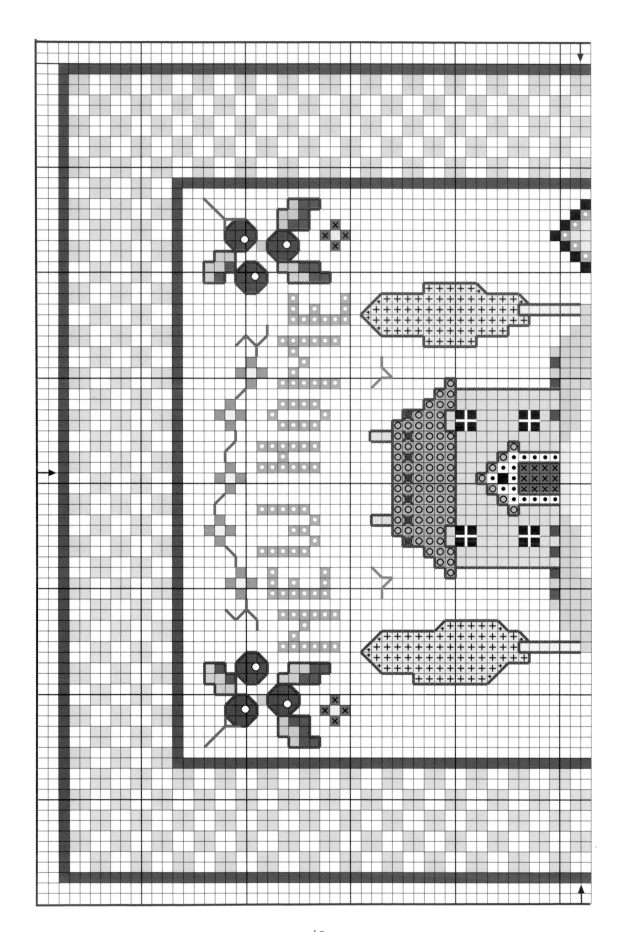

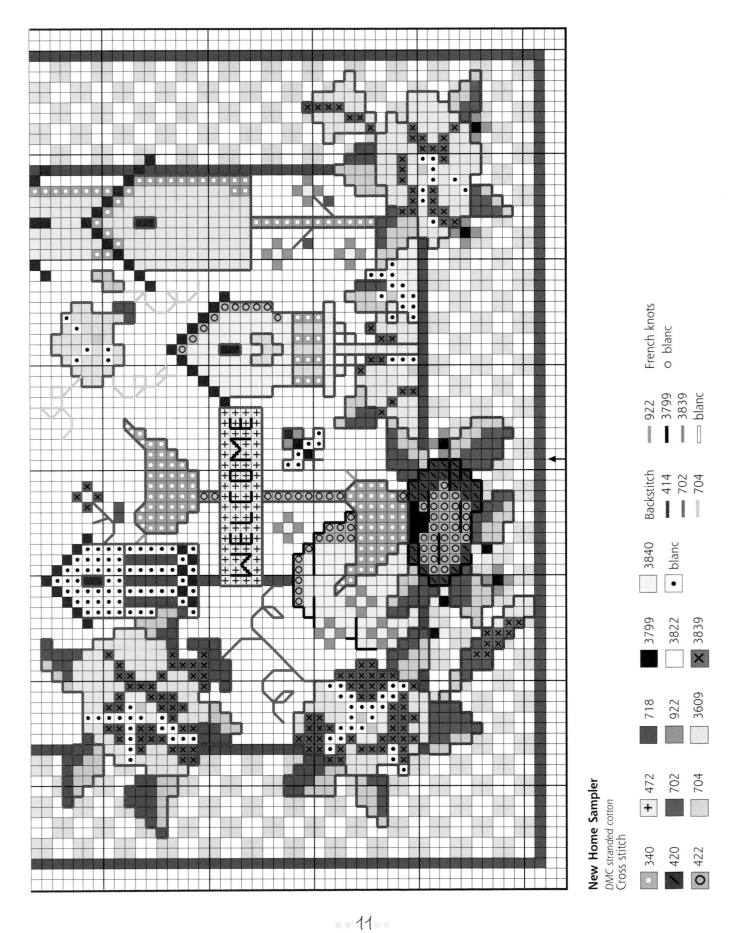

New Home Sampler

DMC stranded cotton
Cross stitch

● 340	+ 472	☐ 3840
◣ 420	◼ 702	● blanc
○ 422	☐ 704	

◼ 718	◼ 3799	◼ 3822
◼ 922	☐ 922	✕ 3839
☐ 3609		

Backstitch
— 414
— 702
— 704

French knots
○ blanc

— 922
— 3799
— 3839
═ blanc

Mother Sampler

This is a beautiful design to stitch for mothers, who will be delighted to receive a hand-stitched picture. The pretty bouquet of spring flowers includes pink tulips, yellow jonquils, white narcissi and bluebells — all tied together with a pink ribbon. There are two little butterflies, with added butterfly charms, while the simple border is stitched in a variegated thread to give a ribbon effect.

YOU WILL NEED

30 x 25cm (12 x 10in) cream
28-count linen or 14-count Aida

DMC stranded cotton (floss)
as in the chart key

Size 26 tapestry needle

Two butterfly charms
(From Debbie Cripps, code
CH4701, see Suppliers)

Stitch count 112 x 86
Design size 20.3 x 15.6cm (8 x 6⅛in)

1 Bind the edges of the fabric or oversew to prevent fraying. Fold the fabric in half, then in half again to find the centre and begin stitching from the centre of the chart overleaf.

2 Use two strands of stranded cotton (floss) for cross stitching and one for the backstitching and outlining. Stitch over two threads of linen or one block of Aida. The border uses pink variegated thread (DMC 48). When stitching with this it is best to complete each whole cross stitch rather than working in rows, to ensure that the colour changes gradually from dark to light.

3 When all the stitching is complete sew on the butterfly charms, if you are using them, with ecru thread, referring to the photograph for positions. Press your work carefully and frame as a picture (see page 98).

Idea
You could make a matching gift tag by stitching a single flower, heart or butterfly from the chart.

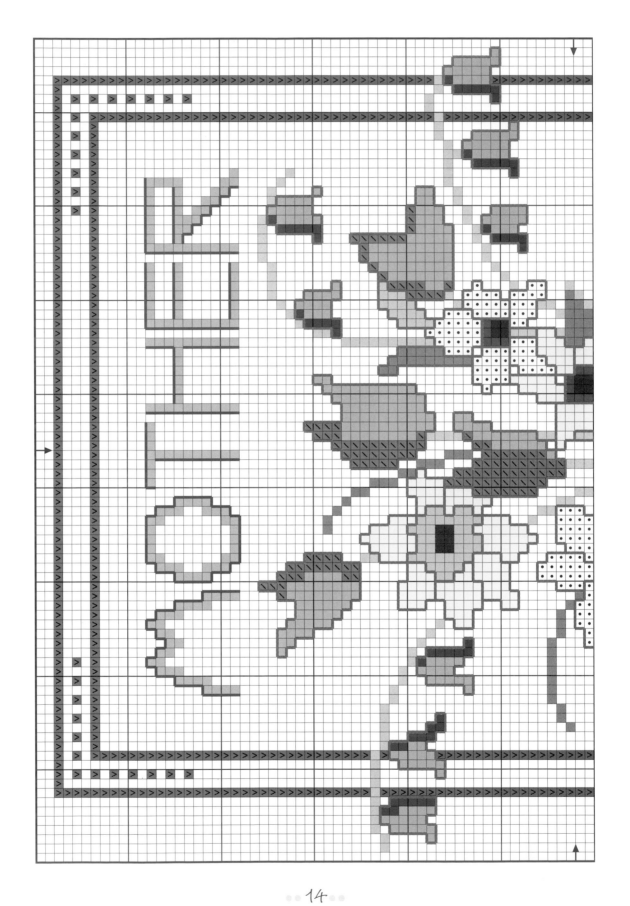

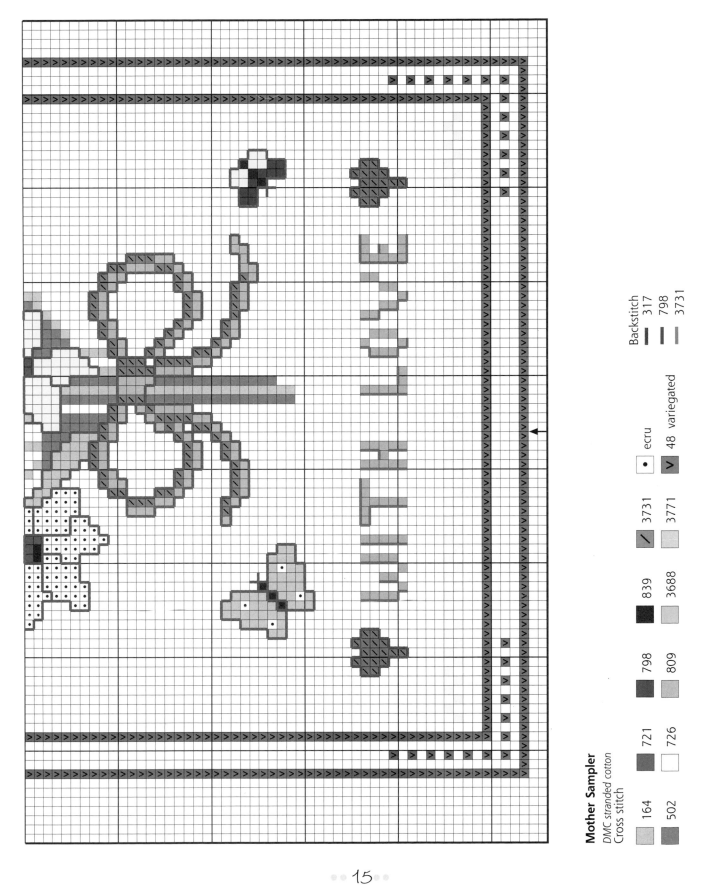

Mother Sampler

DMC stranded cotton
Cross stitch

164	721	798	839	3731
502	726	809	3688	3771

/ 3731	• ecru
3771	V 48 variegated

Backstitch
— 317
— 798
— 3731

New Baby Sampler

This little sampler, suitable for a boy or girl, is easy to stitch and can be made in advance of a baby's birth, with the appropriate name, weight and date added when the baby arrives. The bright rainbow colours have a fresh feel which would look lovely in a baby's room. There are also two new baby cards inspired by this design, in traditional pale blue and pale pink.

YOU WILL NEED

30 x 30cm (10 x 10in)
antique white 14-count Aida
or 28-count linen

DMC stranded cotton (floss)
as in the chart key

Size 26 tapestry needle

Stitch count 80 x 86
Design size 14.5 x 15.6 cm (5¾ x 6⅛in)

1 Bind the edges of the fabric or oversew to prevent fraying. Fold the fabric in half, then in half again to find the centre and begin stitching from the centre of the chart on page 18.

2 Stitch over one block of Aida or two threads of linen, using two strands of stranded cotton (floss) for whole cross stitches and three-quarter cross stitches. Use one strand for the backstitching and outlining. The bunny's eyes are French knots in one strand.

3 Stitch the baby's name, date and weight using the alphabets and numerals charted on page 102. Use a pencil and graph paper to plan the words and numbers correctly before you begin stitching.

4 When all the stitching is complete, press your work carefully and frame as a picture (see page 98 for advice).

Ideas

The various motifs can be stitched separately for cards and gifts like bibs and booties. The simple rainbow checks could be stitched on narrow Aida band and added to a soft white towel.

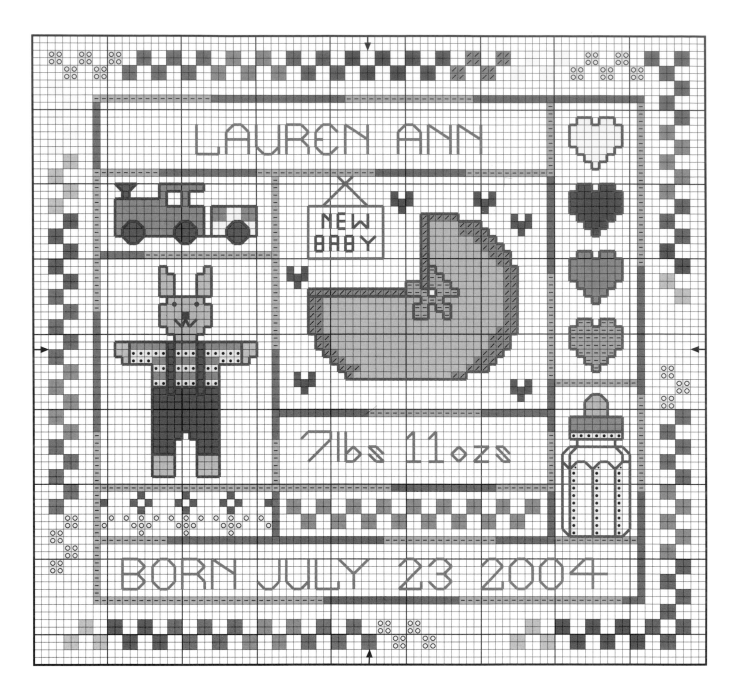

New Baby Sampler

DMC stranded cotton
Cross stitch

■ 317	◯ 472	☐ 726	■ 3328	**Backstitch**	**French knots**
╱ 436	■ 553	■ 156	■ 3812	— 317	● 317
■ 437	— 554	• 3024		— 553	
				— 3812	

New Baby Cards

These sweet little cards are perfect to give on the arrival of a new baby. Stitch the designs on 16 x 14cm (6 x 5½in) pieces of 14-count white Aida. Follow the charts below, using two strands of stranded cotton (floss) for cross stitch and one strand for backstitch and French knots. Mount the finished embroidery into a pale blue or pale pink card with a 7 x 5cm (2¾ x 2in) aperture (see page 99).

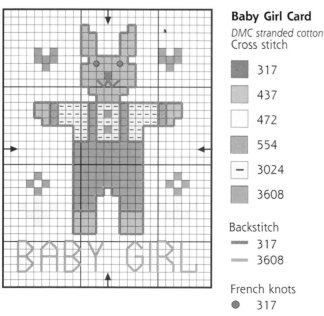

Baby Girl Card

DMC stranded cotton
Cross stitch

■	317
▨	437
□	472
▨	554
−	3024
▨	3608

Backstitch
— 317
— 3608

French knots
● 317

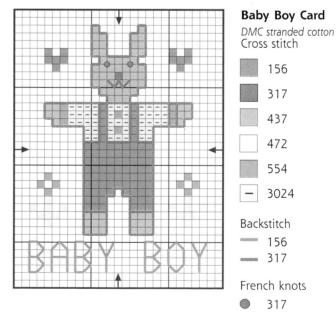

Baby Boy Card

DMC stranded cotton
Cross stitch

▨	156
■	317
▨	437
□	472
▨	554
−	3024

Backstitch
— 156
— 317

French knots
● 317

Stitch counts each 32 x 23
Design sizes each 5.8 x 4.2cm (2¼ x 1⅝in)

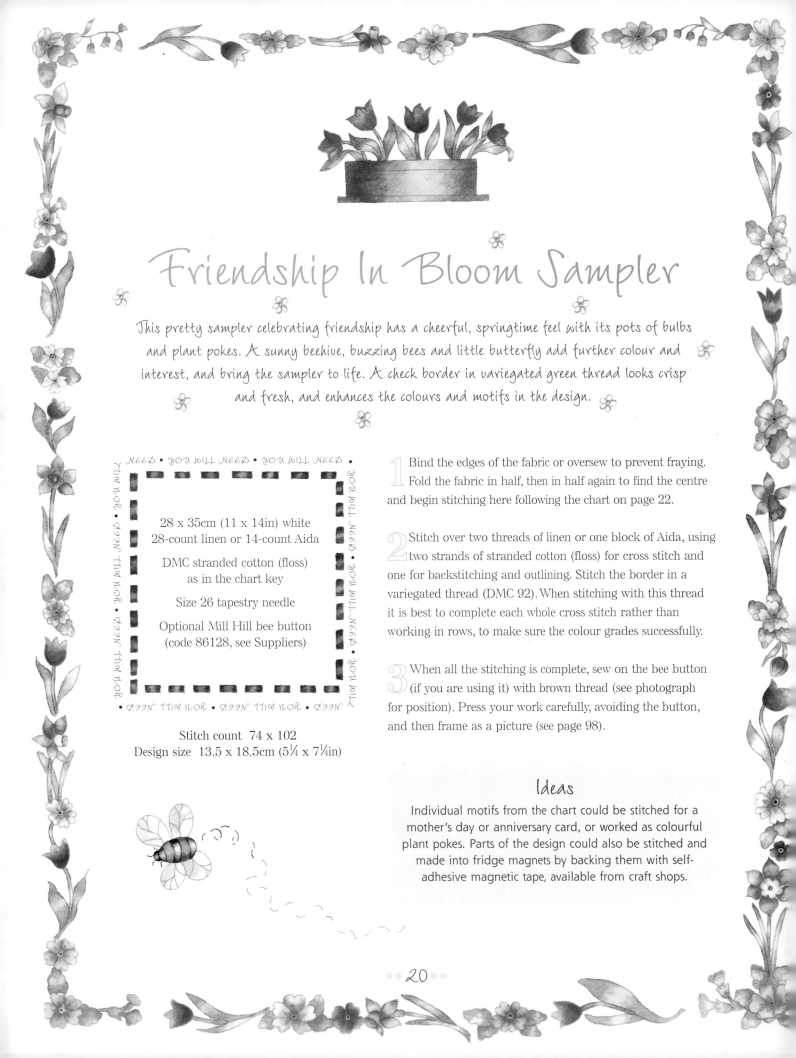

Friendship In Bloom Sampler

This pretty sampler celebrating friendship has a cheerful, springtime feel with its pots of bulbs and plant pokes. A sunny beehive, buzzing bees and little butterfly add further colour and interest, and bring the sampler to life. A check border in variegated green thread looks crisp and fresh, and enhances the colours and motifs in the design.

28 x 35cm (11 x 14in) white
28-count linen or 14-count Aida

DMC stranded cotton (floss)
as in the chart key

Size 26 tapestry needle

Optional Mill Hill bee button
(code 86128, see Suppliers)

Stitch count 74 x 102
Design size 13.5 x 18.5cm (5¼ x 7¼in)

1 Bind the edges of the fabric or oversew to prevent fraying. Fold the fabric in half, then in half again to find the centre and begin stitching here following the chart on page 22.

2 Stitch over two threads of linen or one block of Aida, using two strands of stranded cotton (floss) for cross stitch and one for backstitching and outlining. Stitch the border in a variegated thread (DMC 92). When stitching with this thread it is best to complete each whole cross stitch rather than working in rows, to make sure the colour grades successfully.

3 When all the stitching is complete, sew on the bee button (if you are using it) with brown thread (see photograph for position). Press your work carefully, avoiding the button, and then frame as a picture (see page 98).

Ideas

Individual motifs from the chart could be stitched for a mother's day or anniversary card, or worked as colourful plant pokes. Parts of the design could also be stitched and made into fridge magnets by backing them with self-adhesive magnetic tape, available from craft shops.

Friendship in Bloom

DMC stranded cotton
Cross stitch

╱	351
+	352
✕	436
	704
○	729
	779
	911
	3607
	3609
	3826
•	ecru
V	92 variegated

Backstitch

——	351
——	436
——	502
——	779
——	3607
——	3826

❀ Plant Pokes ❀

These brightly coloured plant pokes (shown on page 21) are very simple to create. They make a floral gift really special and you could change the words to suit the occasion (see other greetings and messages charted on pages 100 and 101).

YOU WILL NEED • YOU WILL NEED • YOU WILL NEED •

Sheet of cream 14-count stitching paper

DMC stranded cotton (floss) as in the chart key

Size 26 tapestry needle

Squares of brightly coloured felt

Pinking shears

Fabric glue or Copydex

Plant sticks
(available from garden centres)

1 Do not cut the stitching paper to size until the design has been embroidered. Stitch the design from the chart using two strands of stranded cotton (floss) for cross stitch and one strand for backstitch.

2 When all the stitching is complete, cut out the design two holes away from the stitching using pinking shears to create a decorative edge. Cut a piece of felt slightly larger than the design and glue it to the back. Allow to dry then attach the stick with glue and leave to dry.

Plant Pokes

DMC stranded cotton
Cross stitch

■ 310	■ 702	■ 741
■ 552	■ 703	■ 3607
■ 554	■ 720	■ 3608

Backstitch
— 317
— 791

Stitch counts   Daffodil 36 x 44
               Tulip 36 x 38
Design sizes   Daffodil 6.5 x 8cm (2½ x 3⅛in)
               Tulip 6.5 x 6.9cm (2½ x 2¾in)

Spring Greetings Cards

Welcome the spring season with this fresh and pretty collection of cards.

Send your Easter greetings in this Easter egg card or the Easter chick card below – both are full of spring hopes and wishes.

Stitch count
52 x 35
Design size
9.4 x 6.4cm
(3³/₄ x 2¹/₂in)

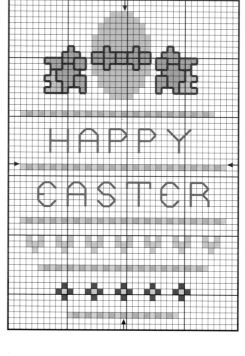

Easter Egg Card

DMC stranded cotton
Cross stitch

	210
	704
	742
	792
	3822

Backstitch
— 317
— 792

Stitch count
36 x 34
Design size
6.5 x 6.2cm
(2¹/₂ x 2¹/₂in)

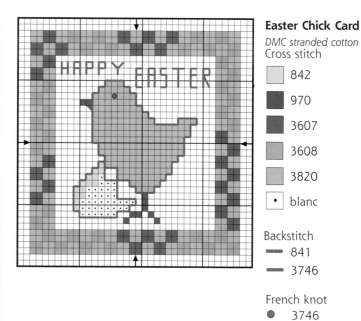

Easter Chick Card

DMC stranded cotton
Cross stitch

	842
	970
	3607
	3608
	3820
•	blanc

Backstitch
— 841
— 3746

French knot
● 3746

Mother's Day Card

DMC stranded cotton
Cross stitch

▨	210
▨	704
▧	956
╱	3689

Backstitch

━	704
━	956

You are sure to delight your mother on mother's day with this delicate floral card in soft lilacs and pinks.

Stitch count
42 x 37
Design size
7.6 x 6.7cm
(3 x 2⅝in)

Get Well Card

DMC stranded cotton
Cross stitch

▦	309
■	317
╱	351
▨	741
I	742
⦁	796
▨	3822
▨	3838

Backstitch

━	317
━	3838

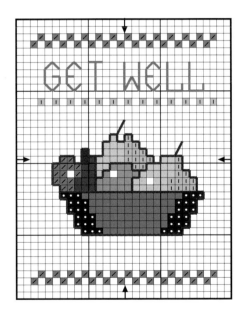

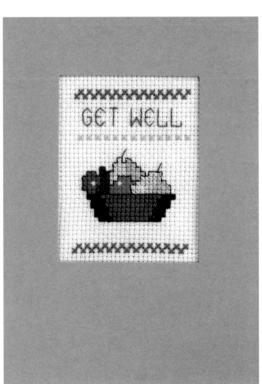

If you know someone who has been ill or in hospital this special hand-stitched get well card will show how much you care and help to speed their recovery.

Stitch count
35 x 26
Design size
9.4 x 4.7cm
(3¾ x 2½in)

Lots of house moves take place in the spring and here is a bright new home card that is perfect for the occasion.

Stitch count
36 x 36
Design size
6.5 x 6.5cm
(2¹/₂ x 2¹/₂in)

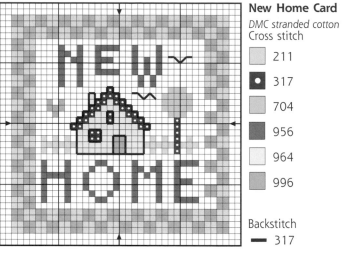

New Home Card

DMC stranded cotton
Cross stitch

	211
⊙	317
	704
	956
	964
	996

Backstitch
— 317

There are two birthday cards in this collection – one with a sea theme and, above right, a pretty floral design.

Stitch count
41 x 40
Design size
7.4 x 7.3cm
(3 x 2⁷/₈in)

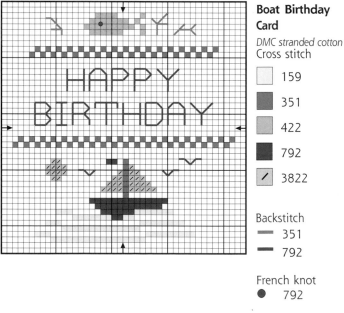

Boat Birthday Card

DMC stranded cotton
Cross stitch

	159
	351
	422
	792
╱	3822

Backstitch
— 351
— 792

French knot
● 792

Floral Birthday Card

DMC stranded cotton

Cross stitch

- ▨ 502
- ▨ 524
- ▨ 742
- ▨ 3609
- ⊡ blanc

Backstitch

— 502
— 3607

Stitch count
41 x 39
Design size
7.4 x 7cm
(3 x 2^3/$_4$in)

St Patrick's Day Card

DMC stranded cotton

Cross stitch

- ▨ 702
- ▨ 704
- ▨ 742
- ⊡ 844

Backstitch

— 844
— 742

At this time of year many people celebrate St Patrick's day, so here is a card to bring a little luck to the recipient on that day.

Stitch count
39 x 31
Design size
7 x 5.6cm
(2^3/$_4$ x 2^1/$_4$in)

Summer

This section is all about sunny days, romantic weddings, lush gardens and happy holidays. There is a delicious wedding sampler, heart-shaped golden and silver wedding anniversary samplers, a glorious garden sampler and a shiny sports car sampler for father's day. The card collection has designs for many summer celebrations, such as weddings, holidays, summer birthdays, July 4th and a thank you teacher card.

Wedding Sampler

A wedding is the perfect occasion to stitch a sampler for, as the bride and groom will be delighted to have a beautiful stitched heirloom as a record of their special day. This sampler will look fresh and modern in today's interiors, but retains some traditional elements. Flowers, wedding bells, hearts and bows capture the romance, a bluebird represents happiness and the words express special wishes for the couple's future together.

35 x 31cm (14 x 12in) cream
28-count linen or 14-count Aida

DMC stranded cotton (floss)
as in the chart key

Size 26 tapestry needle

Mill Hill seed beads in white
(code 00479, see Suppliers)

Beading needle

Stitch count 129 x 104
Design size 23.4 x 19cm (9¼ x 7½in)

1 Begin by working out the names and date you will need to personalize the sampler using the alphabets and numerals on page 102. Use graph paper and a pencil to plan the words and numbers so you can stitch them in the correct positions.

2 Bind the edges of the fabric or oversew to prevent fraying. Fold the fabric in half, then in half again to find the centre and begin stitching here from the centre of the chart overleaf.

3 Stitch over two linen threads or one block of Aida, using two strands of stranded cotton (floss) for cross stitch and French knots, and one for backstitching and outlining. When stitching the date and verse, avoid carrying the thread across the back of the work between the numbers and words as it will show through as dark lines on the front.

4 When all the stitching is complete, sew on the beads with white sewing thread using a beading needle. Press your work carefully and frame as a picture (see page 98).

Ideas

The sampler is easy to stitch and is suitable for the linen I have used or Aida fabric. The pretty motifs can be stitched up quickly for a variety of cards and gifts, such as a pretty ring pillow or a gift bag for a bridesmaid.

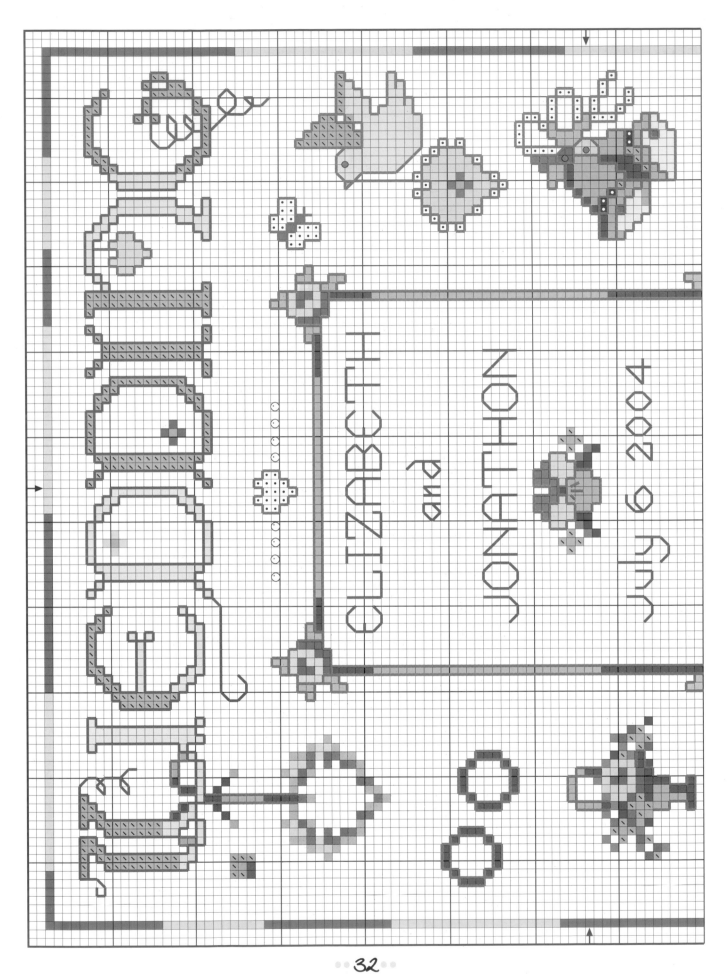

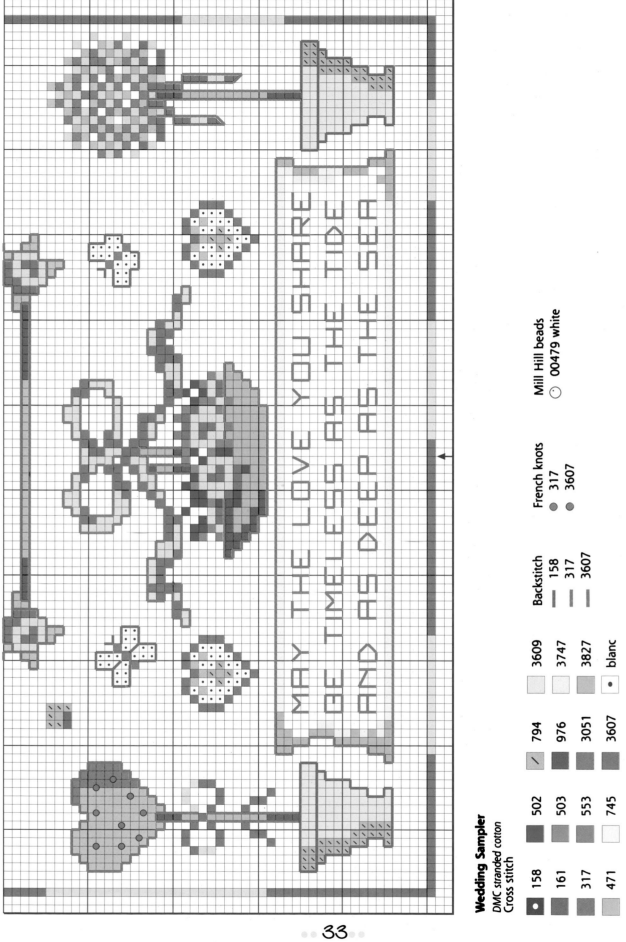

Wedding Sampler
DMC stranded cotton
Cross stitch

158	502	794	3609	
161	503	976	3747	
317	553	3051	3827	
471	745	3607	blanc	

Backstitch
— 158
— 317
— 3607

French knots
● 317
● 3607

Mill Hill beads
⊙ 00479 white

MAY THE LOVE YOU SHARE
BE TIMELESS AS THE TIDE
AND AS DEEP AS THE SEA

Wedding Anniversary Samplers

Stitching a sampler for a special anniversary is a wonderful way of celebrating the occasion. This design has been worked for silver and golden wedding anniversaries, each with appropriate colours, words and numerals. It is a celebration of enduring love and makes a very special gift. The sampler was inspired by traditional band samplers and is designed to fit into a heart-shaped mount — a good picture framer will cut a card mount to shape. The colours are fresh and bright, bringing the traditional style right up to date.

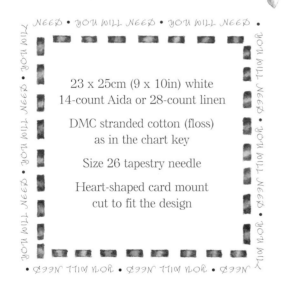

YOU WILL NEED

23 x 25cm (9 x 10in) white
14-count Aida or 28-count linen

DMC stranded cotton (floss)
as in the chart key

Size 26 tapestry needle

Heart-shaped card mount
cut to fit the design

Stitch counts each 66 x 92
Design sizes each 12 x 16.7cm (4¾ x 6½in)

1 Bind the edges of the fabric or oversew to prevent fraying. Fold the fabric in half, then in half again to find the centre and begin stitching from the centre of the chart overleaf.

2 Stitch over two threads of linen or one block of Aida, using two strands of stranded cotton (floss) for cross stitching and one strand for the backstitching and outlining.

3 Stitch the initials and dates of your choice using the alphabet and numerals charted on page 102. Use a pencil and graph paper to plan the words and numbers correctly before you begin stitching. When stitching on pale fabric avoid carrying thread across the back of the work, especially between numbers and words, as the thread will show through as dark lines on the front.

4 When all the stitching is complete press your work carefully and frame as a picture (see page 98 for advice).

Idea

You could easily stitch a matching gift card using motifs like the row of flowers, the roses or the numbers from the chart.

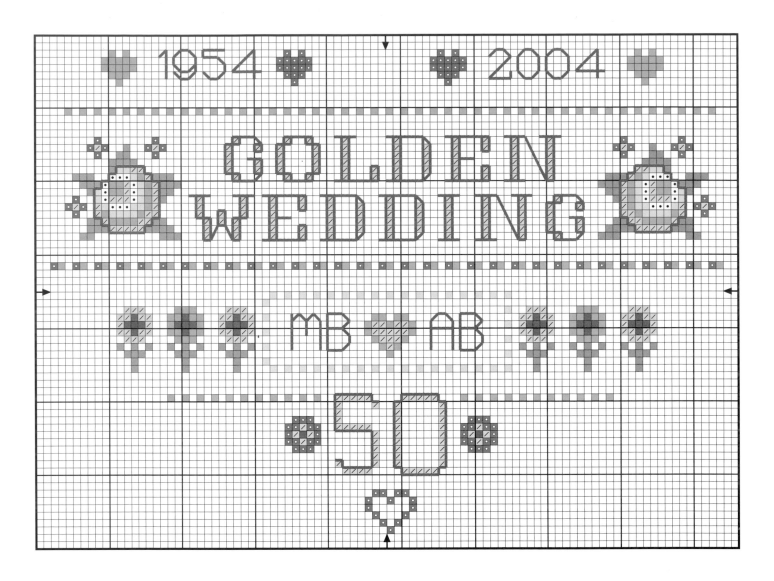

Golden Wedding Anniversary Sampler

DMC stranded cotton
Cross stitch

■ 420	⊡ 720	⊡ ecru
▢ 422	■ 741	
▨ 703	⁄ 742	

Backstitch

— 420

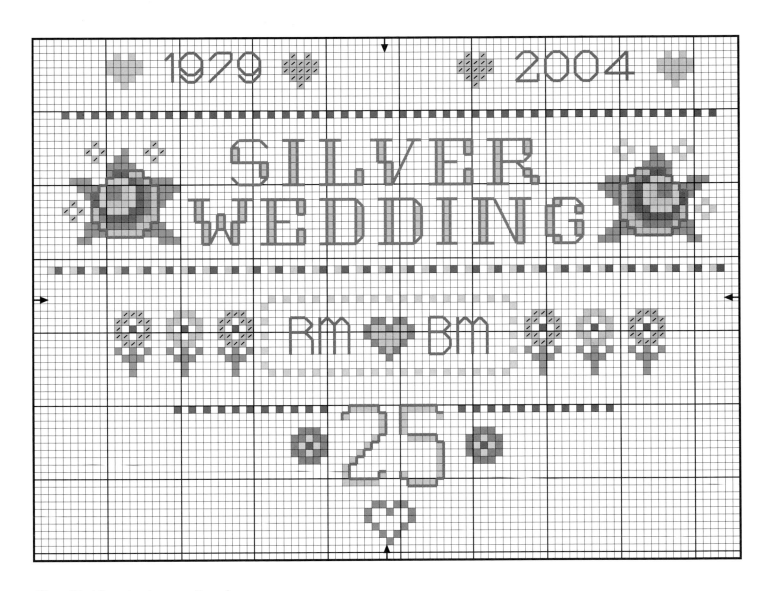

Silver Wedding Anniversary Sampler

DMC stranded cotton
Cross stitch

153		912		Backstitch
208		3838		—— 208
554		3840		—— 3838

Father's Day Sampler

It is often difficult to find a design especially for fathers so here is one for them on their special day. If your father drives a shiny sports car, or dreams of doing so, he is sure to appreciate this picture if you have stitched it just for him. The sports cars, steering wheels and chequered flags are surrounded by a crisp black-and-white-check border, with a golden sun shining above. There is also a sports car card to accompany this design.

30 x 25cm (12 x 10in) white
28-count linen or 14-count Aida

DMC stranded cotton (floss)
as in the chart key

Size 26 tapestry needle

Stitch count 114 x 90
Design size 20.7 x 16.3cm (8³⁄₁₆ x 6⅜in)

1 Bind the edges of the fabric or oversew to prevent fraying. Fold the fabric in half, then in half again to find the centre and begin stitching from the centre of the chart overleaf.

2 Stitch over two threads of linen or one block of Aida, using two strands of stranded cotton (floss) for whole cross stitch and three-quarter cross stitch. Use one strand of black for the backstitching and outlining on the cars, and three strands for the steering wheel of the top car. Use one strand of grey for all other backstitches

3 Personalize the sampler by changing the initials on the number plate using the alphabet and numerals charted on page 102.

4 When all the stitching is complete, press your work carefully and frame as a picture (see page 98 for advice).

Idea
You could use Aida band to decorate towels for dad's gym sessions, stitching the check border, the steering wheels or flags in a row.

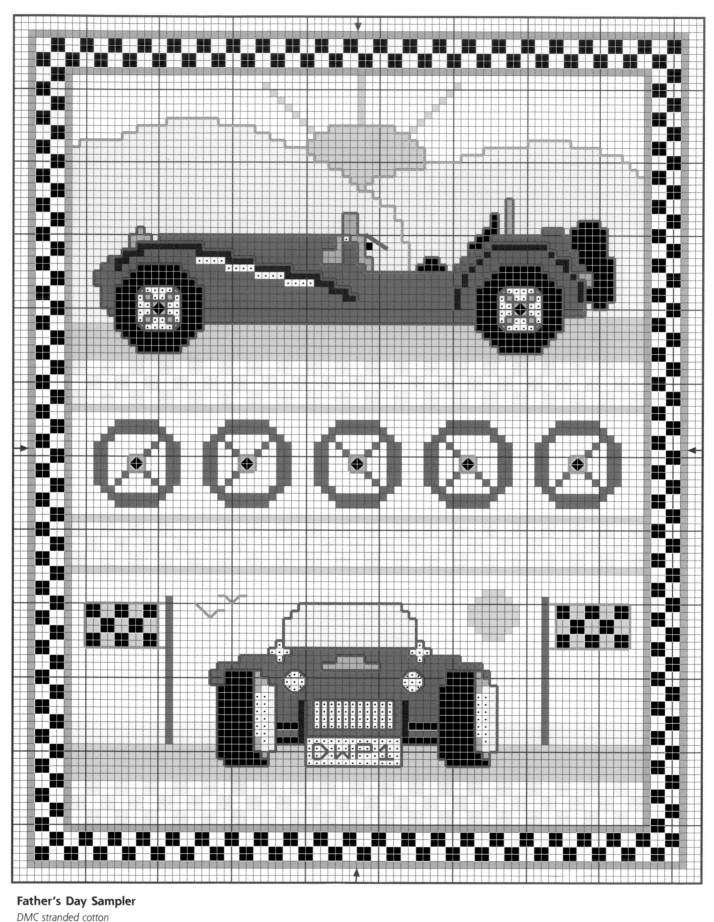

Father's Day Sampler

DMC stranded cotton
Cross stitch

Backstitch

■	310	■	318	□	165	
■	161	■	347	■	996	

□	3024	■	3820	
■	3328	•	blanc	

— 310

— 317

☀ Sports Car Card ☀

This little design makes a great father's day card and would also be suitable
for a birthday card for any car enthusiast.

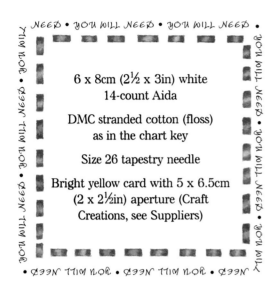

6 x 8cm (2½ x 3in) white
14-count Aida

DMC stranded cotton (floss)
as in the chart key

Size 26 tapestry needle

Bright yellow card with 5 x 6.5cm
(2 x 2½in) aperture (Craft
Creations, see Suppliers)

Stitch count 20 x 27
Design size 3.6 x 4.9cm (1½ x 2in)

1 Start stitching in the centre of the fabric from the centre of
the chart. Work over one block of Aida, using two strands
of stranded cotton (floss) for the cross stitches and three-quarter
cross stitches and one strand for the backstitch outlines.

2 When all the stitching is complete, make up the card
following the instructions on page 99.

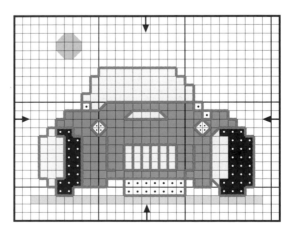

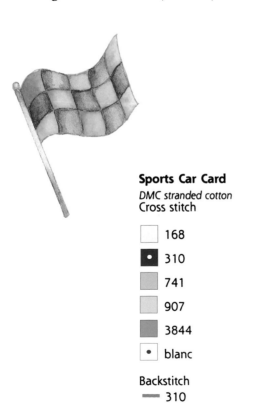

Sports Car Card
DMC stranded cotton
Cross stitch

☐	168
⊡	310
☐	741
☐	907
☐	3844
•	blanc

Backstitch
— 310

Gardener's Sampler

This sampler was designed to be bright and filled with lots of gardening images — from the potting shed with tools, herbs hanging up to dry and apples stored in trays, to the beehives, birdhouses and big sunflowers. Garden wildlife is not forgotten either, with robins, butterflies and lots of buzzing bees. Bright flowers, vegetables, seed packets and a watering-can complete this cheerful sampler with its hopeful words that gardeners will appreciate.

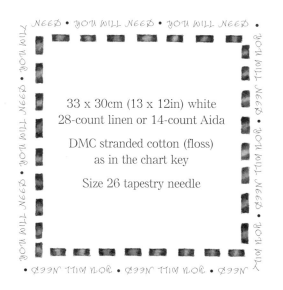

NEED • YOU WILL NEED • YOU WILL NEED

33 x 30cm (13 x 12in) white
28-count linen or 14-count Aida

DMC stranded cotton (floss)
as in the chart key

Size 26 tapestry needle

Stitch count 130 x 114
Design size 23.5 x 20.7cm (9¼ x 8⅛in)

1 Bind the edges of the fabric or oversew to prevent fraying. Fold the fabric in half, then in half again to find the centre and begin stitching from the centre of the chart overleaf.

2 Stitch over two threads of linen or one block of Aida, using two strands of stranded cotton (floss) for cross stitches and three-quarter cross stitches. Use one strand for backstitching and outlining and one strand for the French knots for the robins' eyes.

3 When all the stitching is complete, press your work carefully and frame as a picture (see page 98 for advice).

Ideas

Many of the motifs in this design are suitable for cards and small gifts for gardeners, for example to decorate treat bags, towel bands and gardening gloves.

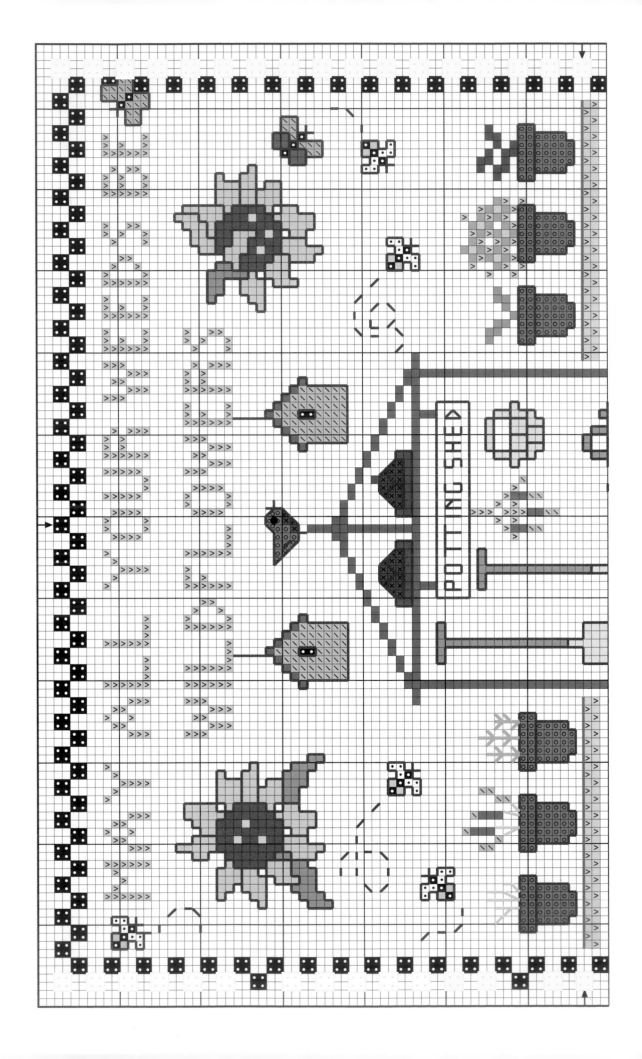

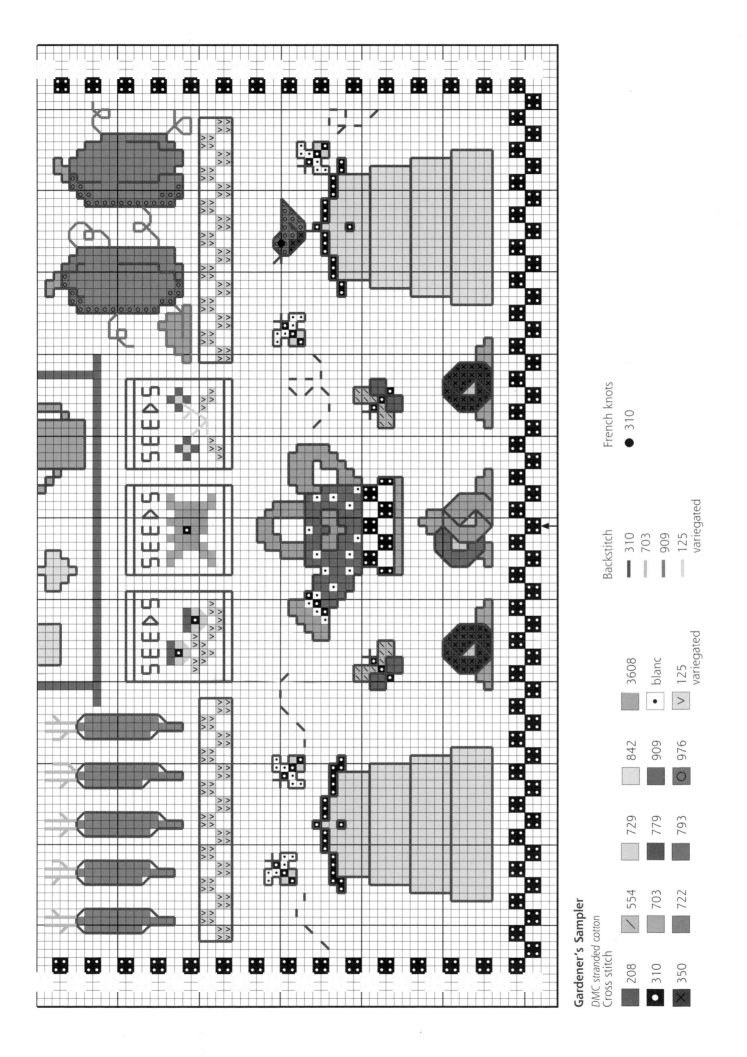

Gardener's Sampler

DMC stranded cotton
Cross stitch

	208		554		729		842		3608
	310		703		779		909	•	blanc
	350		722		793	O	976	V	125
									variegated

Backstitch
— 310
— 703
— 909
— 125
variegated

French knots
● 310

Summer Greetings Cards

Here is a selection of cheerful cards to celebrate summer occasions.

The end of the school year is the perfect time to make this simple but attractive little card to give to your child's teacher as a special thank you.

Stitch count
42 x 41
Design size
7.6 x 7.6cm
(3 x 3in)

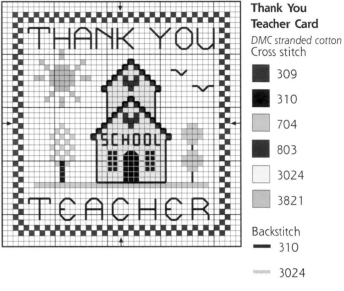

Thank You Teacher Card

DMC stranded cotton
Cross stitch

■	309
■	310
▨	704
■	803
▨	3024
▨	3821

Backstitch

—	310
—	3024

To wish family and friends a happy holiday, why not stitch them one of these holiday cards? They could also be made up as little pictures, as mementoes of a family trip.

Stitch count
41 x 33
Design size
7.6 x 6cm
(3 x 2⅜in)

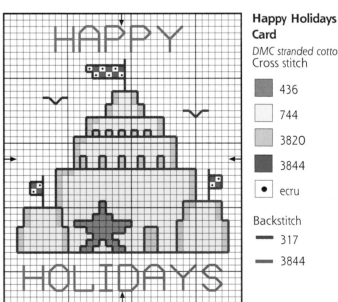

Happy Holidays Card

DMC stranded cotton
Cross stitch

▨	436
▨	744
▨	3820
▨	3844
•	ecru

Backstitch

—	317
—	3844

Stitching Notes: Work the designs on 14-count white Aida with two strands of stranded cotton (floss) for cross stitch and one for backstitch. See page 99 for making up cards and page 100 for a selection of charted messages.

Palm Tree Card

DMC stranded cotton
Cross stitch

☐	90 variegated
▨	436
▨	703
▨	840
▨	3846

Backstitch
— 317

This card could be sent to someone planning to visit somewhere exotic. Or why not stitch one for yourself with the date, as a souvenir of a memorable trip of your own?

Stitch count
57 x 33
Design size
10 x 6cm
(4 x 2³⁄₈in)

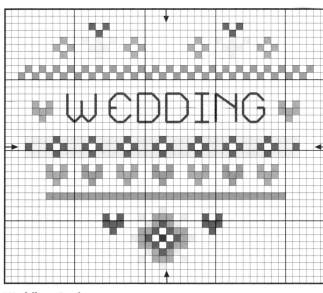

Here is the prettiest wedding card, with tiny bands of pattern in fondant colours contained in a heart-shaped card – perfect to stitch or to receive.

Stitch count
42 x 35
Design size
7.6 x 6.3cm
(3 x 2¹⁄₂in)

Wedding Card

DMC stranded cotton
Cross stitch

					Backstitch	
☐	165	▨	552	▨ 3608	—	552
▨	340	▨	3607			

Using bands of cross stitch in a similar way to the wedding card, this quick to stitch design would be ideal for a wedding anniversary.

Stitch count
45 x 44
Design size
8 x 8cm
(3¼ x 3¼in)

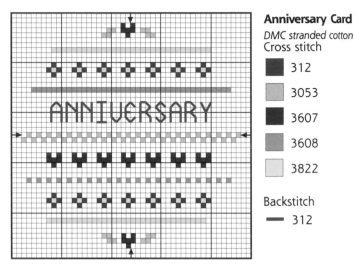

Anniversary Card
DMC stranded cotton
Cross stitch

312
3053
3607
3608
3822

Backstitch
312

This bright little card with its flag flying proudly, is easy to stitch and perfect to give in celebration of American Independence Day.

Stitch count
33 x 23
Design size
6 x 4cm
(2⅜ x 1⅝in)

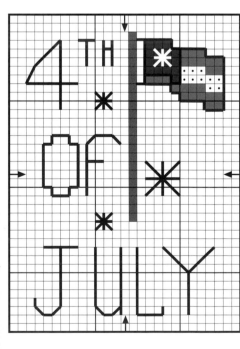

4th of July Card
DMC stranded cotton
Cross stitch

351
796
420
blanc

Backstitch
351
796
blanc

Blue Candles
Cake Card

DMC stranded cotton
Cross stitch

▨	741
☐	744
■	995
▩	996
▨	3687
•	blanc

Backstitch

—	317
—	996

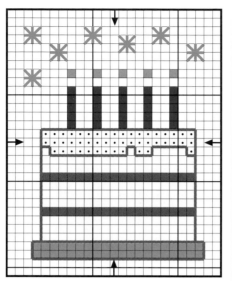

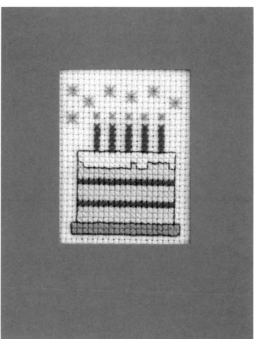

These two delicious cake cards to stitch for children complete this collection. One has blue candles for a boy and the other has pink – perfect for a little girl.

Stitch count
27 x 21
Design size
5 x 3.8cm
(2 x 1½in)

Pink Candles
Cake Card

DMC stranded cotton
Cross stitch

▨	605
▨	741
☐	744
▨	964
▨	3687

Backstitch

—	317

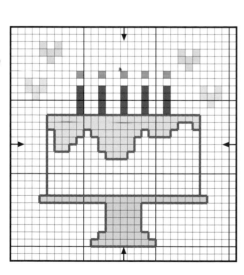

Stitch count
28 x 27
Design size
5 x 5cm
(2 x 2in)

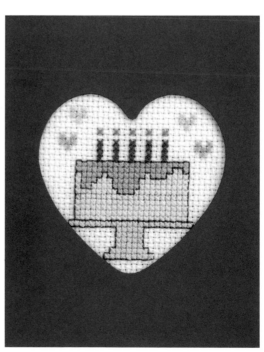

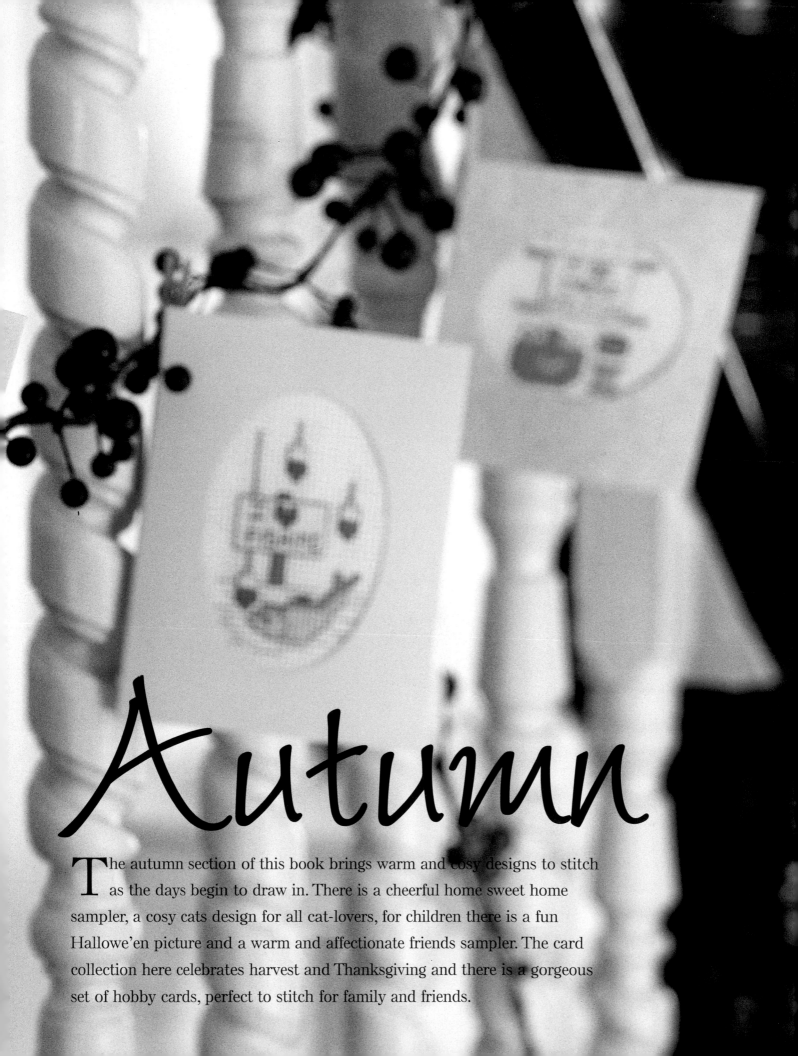

Autumn

The autumn section of this book brings warm and cosy designs to stitch as the days begin to draw in. There is a cheerful home sweet home sampler, a cosy cats design for all cat-lovers, for children there is a fun Hallowe'en picture and a warm and affectionate friends sampler. The card collection here celebrates harvest and Thanksgiving and there is a gorgeous set of hobby cards, perfect to stitch for family and friends.

Home Sweet Home Sampler

This sampler was inspired by the wonderful 1930s pottery of Clarice Cliff, its bold designs and vibrant colours, which were amazingly innovative at the time. The pleasure of working with vivid colours is an enjoyable part of designing for me, and I especially loved the turquoise shades in this sampler. A Home Sweet Home sampler used to hang in many houses in the days when schoolgirls stitched as part of their education. This sampler reaffirms that tradition in a bright, contemporary way.

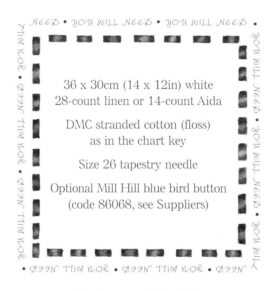

36 x 30cm (14 x 12in) white
28-count linen or 14-count Aida

DMC stranded cotton (floss)
as in the chart key

Size 26 tapestry needle

Optional Mill Hill blue bird button
(code 86068, see Suppliers)

Stitch count 139 x 119
Design size 25.2 x 21.5cm (10 x 8½in)

1 Bind the edges of the fabric or oversew to prevent fraying. Fold the fabric in half, then in half again to find the centre and begin stitching from the centre of the chart overleaf.

2 Stitch over two threads of linen or one block of Aida, using two strands of stranded cotton (floss) for whole cross stitches and three-quarter cross stitches and one strand for all the backstitching and outlining.

3 When all the stitching is complete, sew on the blue bird button, if you are using it, with dark turquoise thread (see photograph for position). Press your work carefully, avoiding the button, and frame as a picture (see page 98).

Ideas

There are many motifs in the design that could be used in other ways, for example, the teapots could be stitched on Aida band and used to edge tea towels, the vases of flowers and the teapots could be used on cards and the central scene would make a sweet little picture.

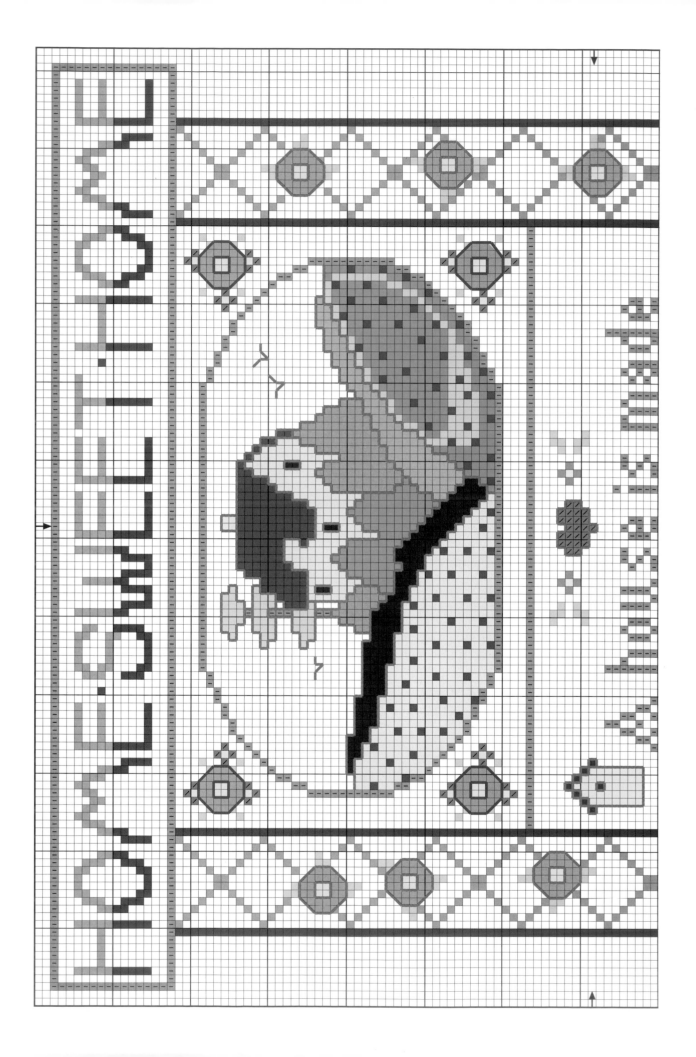

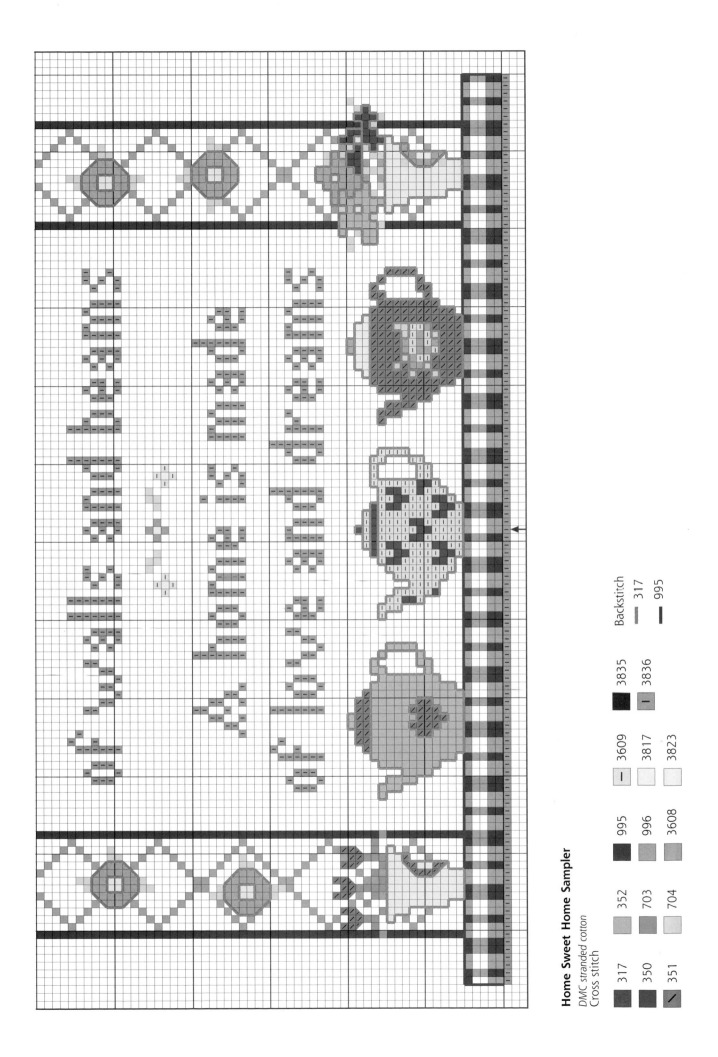

Home Sweet Home Sampler

DMC stranded cotton
Cross stitch

317	995	3609	3835
352	996	3817	3836
350	703	3823	
351	704	3608	

Backstitch
— 317
— 995

Hallowe'en Fun Sampler

This design is a lively celebration of Hallowe'en and all things spooky. There is a friendly ghost, pumpkin lantern, bats and spiders to help conjure up some Hallowe'en fun. There are two Mill Hill buttons in the design or you could stitch the motifs from the chart instead if you prefer. There are also two accompanying cards.

Stitch count 58 x 109
Design size 10.5 x 19.8cm (4⅛ x 7¾in)

1 Bind the edges of the fabric or oversew to prevent fraying. Fold the fabric in half, then in half again to find the centre and begin stitching from the centre of the chart on page 58.

2 Stitch over two threads of linen or one block of Aida, using two strands of stranded cotton (floss) for cross stitches and three-quarter cross stitches. Use one strand for backstitching and outlining.

3 When all the stitching is complete, sew on the buttons if you are using them (see photograph for positions) or stitch the motifs from the chart instead. Press your work carefully, avoiding the buttons, and frame as a picture (see page 98).

Ideas

Motifs from this design could be stitched as patches on to a ready-made bag filled with goodies for trick or treating. Alternatively, fray the edges of the patches and glue to a little basket.

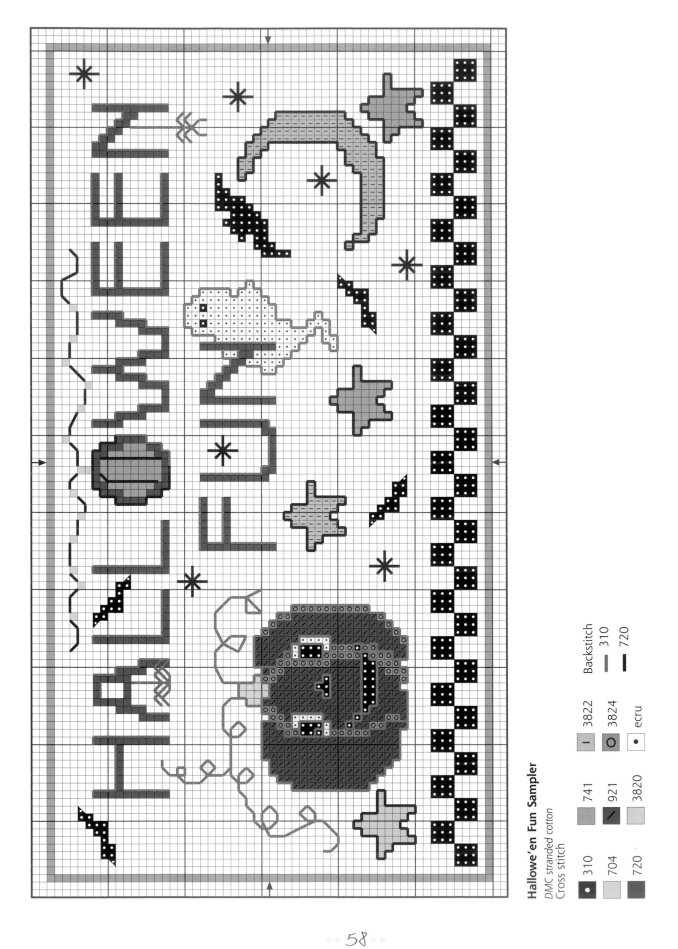

Hallowe'en Fun Sampler

DMC stranded cotton
Cross stitch

⊡ 310	▨ 741	∣ 3822		Backstitch
▨ 704	◢ 921	⊙ 3824		— 310
▨ 720	∙ 3820	⊡ ecru		— 720

⭐ Hallowe'en Cards ⭐

These little cards are great fun to stitch for Hallowe'en. Stitch the designs on 10 x 10cm (4 x 4in) pieces of 14-count white Aida, using two strands of stranded cotton (floss) for cross stitch and one strand for backstitch and French knots. Work the stars in one strand and star stitch (see page 98). Mount into cards with circular apertures of 6.5 x 6.5cm (2½ x 2½in) – see page 99 for instructions.

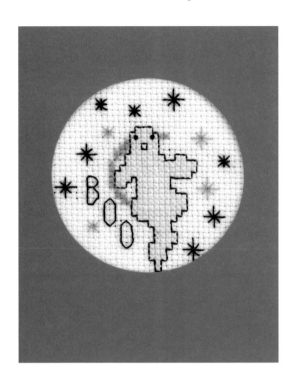

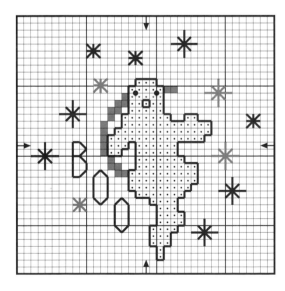

Hallowe'en Cards
DMC stranded cotton
Cross stitch

⬛	310
⬛	722
⬚	ecru

Backstitch and star stitch

— 310
— 722

French knots

● 310

Stitch counts   Boo 33 x 33
                   Hat 29 x 27
Design sizes   Boo 6 x 6cm (2⅜ x 2⅜in)
                   Hat 5 x 5cm (2 x 2in)

Cosy Cats Sampler

This design was inspired by an Eleanor Farjeon poem well known among cat lovers called 'Cats Sleep Anywhere'. It wittily lists all the places a cat may be found sleeping — literally anywhere! It is the perfect design to curl up and stitch on a chilly autumn evening, with its cosy sleeping cats and warm colours. It is quick and simple to work, with a narrow patchwork border enclosing the design which is in the form of a long, narrow band sampler.

35.5 x 18cm (14 x 7in) cream 28-count linen or 14-count Aida

DMC stranded cotton (floss) as in the chart key

Size 26 tapestry needle

1 Bind the edges of the fabric or oversew to prevent fraying. Fold the fabric in half, then in half again to find the centre and begin stitching from the centre of the chart overleaf.

2 Stitch over two threads of linen or one block of Aida, using two strands of stranded cotton (floss) for cross stitches and three-quarter cross stitches. Use one strand for backstitching and outlining.

3 When all the stitching is complete, press your work carefully and frame as a picture (see page 98). Alternatively, you could hem the design around the edges and hang it from a wire hanger – perhaps one featuring a cat.

Stitch count 148 x 48
Design size 27 x 8.7cm (10½ x 3½in)

Ideas
The individual cats would make lovely motifs for greetings cards for your cat-loving friends or family.

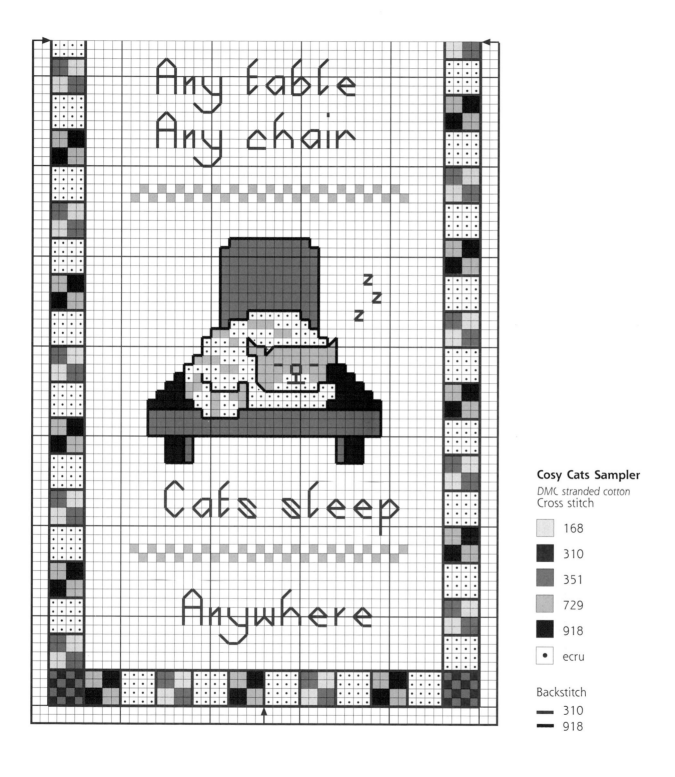

Cosy Cats Sampler

DMC stranded cotton
Cross stitch

▫	168
■	310
■	351
▨	729
■	918
•	ecru

Backstitch
— 310
— 918

Friends Sampler

This sweet little sampler is in a folk art-style and celebrates friendship in soft, pretty colours. It would be a lovely gift for a special friend. It is quick and easy to stitch, uses only whole cross stitch and backstitch, and is suitable for the linen I have used or for Aida fabric. There are two optional star buttons or you could stitch the star motifs from the chart instead. The little figures, house or checked hearts could be stitched for greetings cards.

30 x 23cm (12 x 9in) antique
white 28-count linen
or 14-count Aida

DMC stranded cotton (floss)
as in the chart key

Size 26 tapestry needle

Optional Mill Hill buttons,
two blue stars (code 86240,
see Suppliers)

Stitch count 109 x 65
Design size 20 x 11.8cm (7¾ x 4⅝in)

1 Bind the edges of the fabric or oversew to prevent fraying. Fold the fabric in half, then in half again to find the centre and begin stitching from the centre of the chart overleaf.

2 Stitch over two threads of linen or one block of Aida, using two strands of stranded cotton (floss) for cross stitching and one strand for the backstitching and outlining.

3 When all the stitching is complete, use matching thread to sew on the two star buttons, if you are using them (see photograph for position), or stitch the star motifs with one strand in star stitch instead (see page 98). Press your work carefully, avoiding the buttons, and then frame as a picture (see page 98).

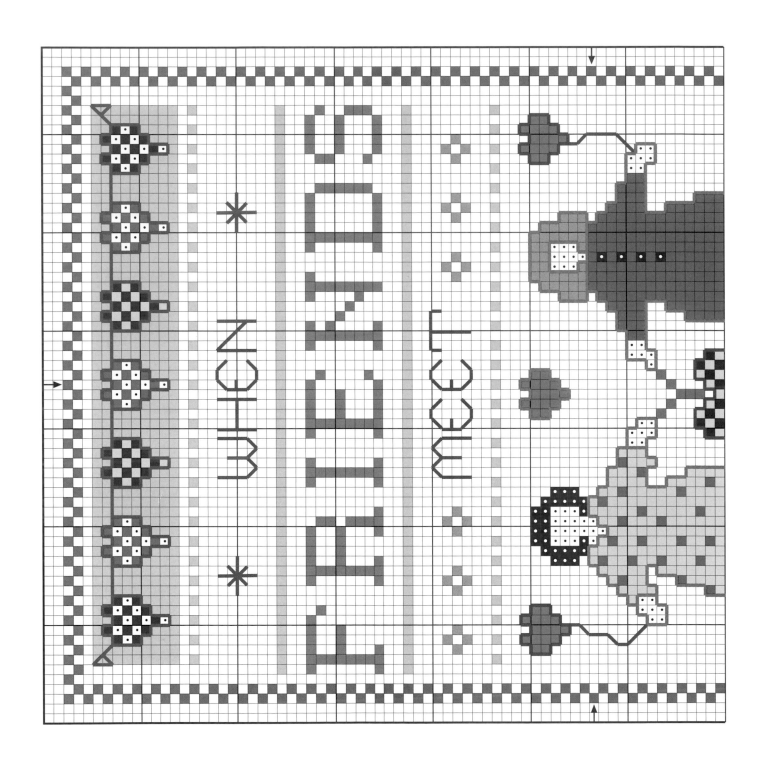

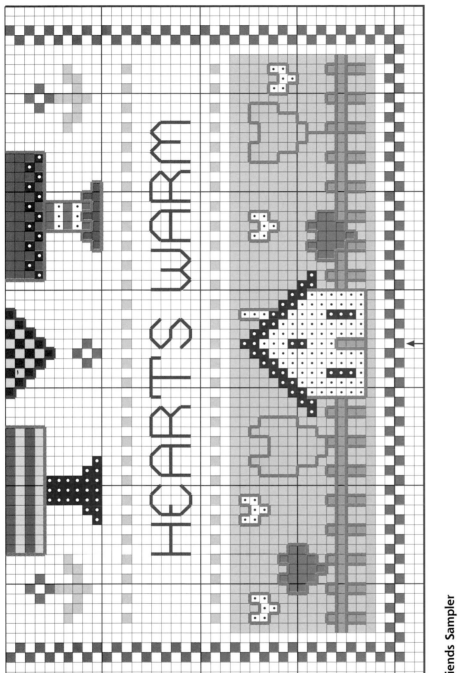

Friends Sampler

DMC stranded cotton
Cross stitch

310	721	964	3846
436	761	3687	blanc
704	803	3812	

Backstitch

— 317
— 803

Autumn Greetings Cards

This card collection includes harvest and Thanksgiving cards and a set of hobby cards.

In this card, a basketful of tasty fruits and vegetables and a simple message mark the harvest safely gathered in.

Stitch count
28 x 39
Design size
5 x 7cm
(2 x 2³⁄₄in)

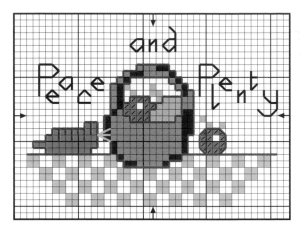

Harvest Card

DMC stranded cotton
Cross stitch

			Backstitch
✎ 351	704	3822	▬ 310
434	722		▬ 317
436	809		▬ 704

This design features all sorts of bright fruits in a bowl making it a cheerful card to give on Thanksgiving Day.

Stitch count
23 x 31
Design size
4.2 x 5.6cm
(1⁵⁄₈ x 2¹⁄₄in)

Happy Thanksgiving Card

DMC stranded cotton
Cross stitch

			Backstitch
310	721	3820	▬ 310
317	809		▬ 317
703	✎ 3328		

Stitching Notes: Work the designs on 14-count white Aida with two strands of stranded cotton (floss) for cross stitch and one for backstitch. See page 99 for making up cards and page 100 for a selection of charted messages.

I Love Cross Stitch Card

DMC stranded cotton
Cross stitch

- 153
- 436
- 809
- 3822
- • ecru

Backstitch

- 153
- 310
- 317
- 809

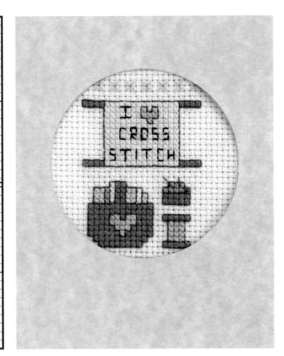

The work basket, cotton reel and pincushion motifs in this card are easy to stitch. You could also stitch the design as a little picture for your sewing room wall.

Stitch count
35 x 23
Design size
6.3 x 4.2cm
(2½ x 1⅝in)

I Love Quilts Card

DMC stranded cotton
Cross stitch

- 351
- 436
- 502
- 809
- • ecru

Backstitch

- 310
- 317

This charming little card, with its distinctive patchwork pattern, is ideal to give to a stitching friend who is a fan of quilting.

Stitch count
38 x 28
Design size
7 x 5cm
(2¾ x 2in)

If you know a keen cook, why not stitch this card for their birthday? You could make a matching gift tag using just the striped bowl.

Stitch count
35 x 25
Design size
6.3 x 4.5cm
(2 1/2 x 1 3/4in)

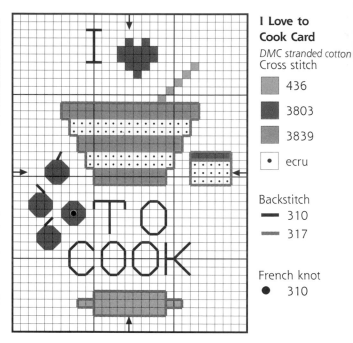

I Love to Cook Card

DMC stranded cotton
Cross stitch

▨	436
▨	3803
▨	3839
•	ecru

Backstitch
— 310
— 317

French knot
● 310

With its beehive, potted plant and vegetables, this card is bright and cheerful and is sure to please anyone with green fingers.

Stitch count
33 x 25
Design size
6 x 4.5cm
(2 3/8 x 1 3/4in)

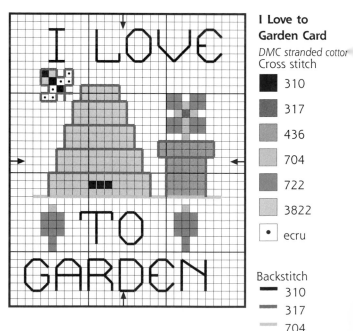

I Love to Garden Card

DMC stranded cotton
Cross stitch

■	310
▨	317
▨	436
▨	704
▨	722
▨	3822
•	ecru

Backstitch
— 310
— 317
— 704

I Love Sailing Card

DMC stranded cotton
Cross stitch

▨	318
■	333
■	351
▨	809
•	ecru

Backstitch

—	310
—	317

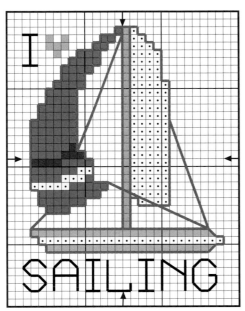

This simple little card with its stylish sailing boat in fresh colours is sure to please someone whose hobby is sailing.

Stitch count
34 x 26
Design size
6.2 x 4.7cm
(2$\frac{1}{2}$ x 1$\frac{7}{8}$in)

I Love Fishing Card

DMC stranded cotton
Cross stitch

■	317
▨	436
■	502
■	3328
▨	3813
•	ecru

Backstitch

—	310
—	317
—	502

French knot

●	310

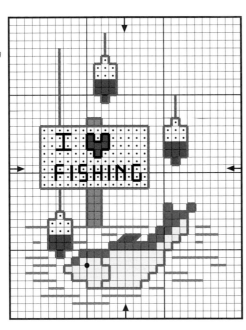

Featuring a wriggling fish and bobbing floats, this card is very quick to stitch – perfect for dads who love to fish.

Stitch count
35 x 26
Design size
6.3 x 4.7cm
(2$\frac{1}{2}$ x 1$\frac{7}{8}$in)

Winter

Winter is a wonderful time for stitching, and this section has lots of festive and snowy designs to celebrate the season in style. There is a charming advent calendar, a cute gingerbread kids sampler and Christmas angels bringing cheer to a picture and a matching bell pull. For the New Year there is an inspirational sampler with a message of hope for the future. The card designs here are a wonderful selection of festive greetings – from Christmas trees to angels and snowmen.

Advent Calendar

An advent calendar, with little parcels containing sweets or tiny treats for each day of December until Christmas Day, is a favourite festive decoration for many families. This one is very quick and easy to stitch and is suitable for Aida as shown here, or linen if preferred. The small, round brass rings are available from haberdashers and soft furnishings departments.

35 x 35cm (14 x 14in) beige
14-count Aida

DMC stranded cotton (floss)
as in the chart key

Size 26 tapestry needle

25 small brass rings

Stitch count 135 x 139
Design size 24.5 x 25.2cm (9⅝ x 10in)

1 Bind the edges of the fabric or oversew to prevent fraying. Fold the fabric in half, then in half again to find the centre and begin stitching from the centre of the chart overleaf.

2 Work over one block of Aida or over two threads of linen, using two strands of stranded cotton (floss) for cross stitching and one for the backstitching and outlining. Count the squares carefully when spacing the numbers.

3 When all the stitching is completed, press your work carefully before sewing on the brass rings over the numbers with red thread. Frame as a picture (see page 98) or make up into a wall hanging (see below).

Ideas

Make the design up into a wall hanging by backing it with cotton fabric, attaching brass rings along the top and hanging it from a wooden pole or brass rod. The central panel of the design could be stitched separately to make a smaller Christmas picture.

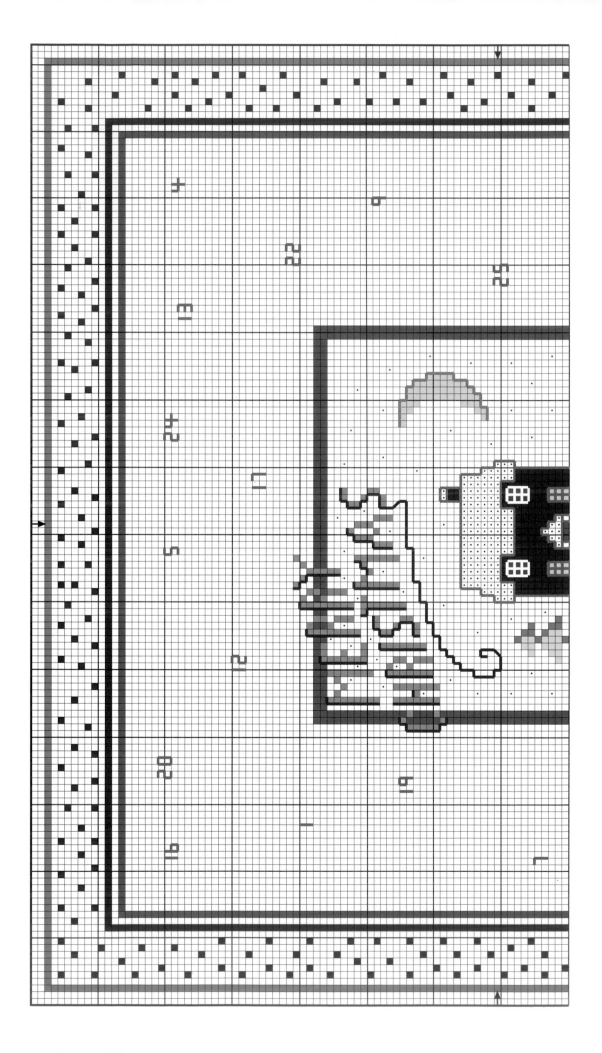

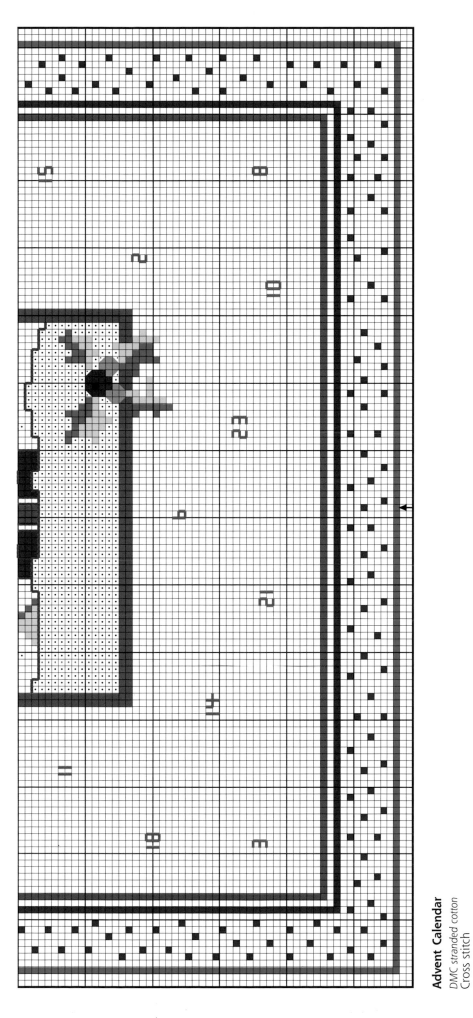

Advent Calendar

DMC stranded cotton
Cross stitch

317	704	3821
350	792	• blanc
702	970	

Backstitch
317 — 970
350 — blanc
792

Gingerbread Kids Sampler

Children love gingerbread men and these days they are available all year round and wearing all kinds of imaginative costumes. This fun sampler shows gingerbread kids all dressed up for winter in their stripy woolly hats and scarves. The colourful holly sprigs and red hearts make this a very cheerful and festive design. I've used a gingerbread man button in the centre but you could stitch the charted motif instead.

23 x 23cm (9 x 9in) white 14-count Aida or 28-count linen

DMC stranded cotton (floss) as in the chart key

Size 26 tapestry needle

Optional Mill Hill gingerbread man button (code 86156, see Suppliers)

Stitch count 75 x 75
Design size 13.6 x 13.6cm (5⅜ x 5⅜in)

1 Bind the edges of the fabric or oversew to prevent fraying. Fold the fabric in half, then in half again to find the centre, count down to the nearest red stitch (if using a button in the centre) and begin stitching here following the chart overleaf.

2 Stitch over one block of Aida or two threads of linen, using two strands of stranded cotton (floss) for cross stitching and the white backstitching. Use two strands for the French knot eyes and the buttons on the gingerbread kids.

3 When all the stitching is complete, sew on the button with white thread, if you are using it, or stitch the motif from the chart instead. Press your work carefully and frame as a picture (see page 98).

Ideas

The individual gingerbread kids motifs would fit neatly into square gift cards. You could use up odds and ends of threads to stitch each one in a different colour combination.

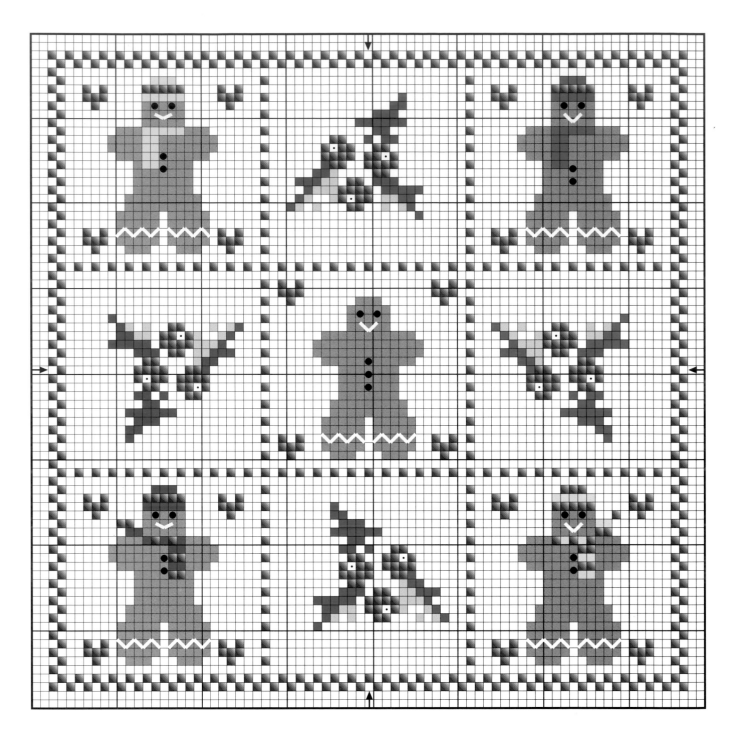

Gingerbread Kids Sampler

DMC stranded cotton
Cross stitch

▓ 167	▒ 743	**Backstitch**	**French knots**
▓ 701	⊡ blanc	▭ blanc	● 310
▒ 704	▓ 57 variegated		

Gingerbread Ornaments

These sweet little gingerbread men are easy to make and look lovely on the Christmas tree or several strung together as a garland. You could make your own versions using up odds and ends of thread and adding buttons, bows or beads.

1 Do not cut the stitching paper until you have embroidered the design. Follow the chart below, using two strands of stranded cotton (floss) for cross stitching and one for backstitching and outlining. When all the stitching is complete, use matching thread to sew on the bell or the button in the position shown in the photograph.

2 Glue the stitched design on to thin card using fabric glue and leave to dry. Cut out the design one hole away from the stitching all the way round. Glue ribbon on to the back to hang the ornament.

Stitch counts 37 x 26
Design sizes 6.7 x 4.7cm (2⅝ x 1⅞in)

Gingerbread Ornaments

DMC stranded cotton
Cross stitch

■	310
▨	436
▨	907
■	3801

Backstitch
— 310

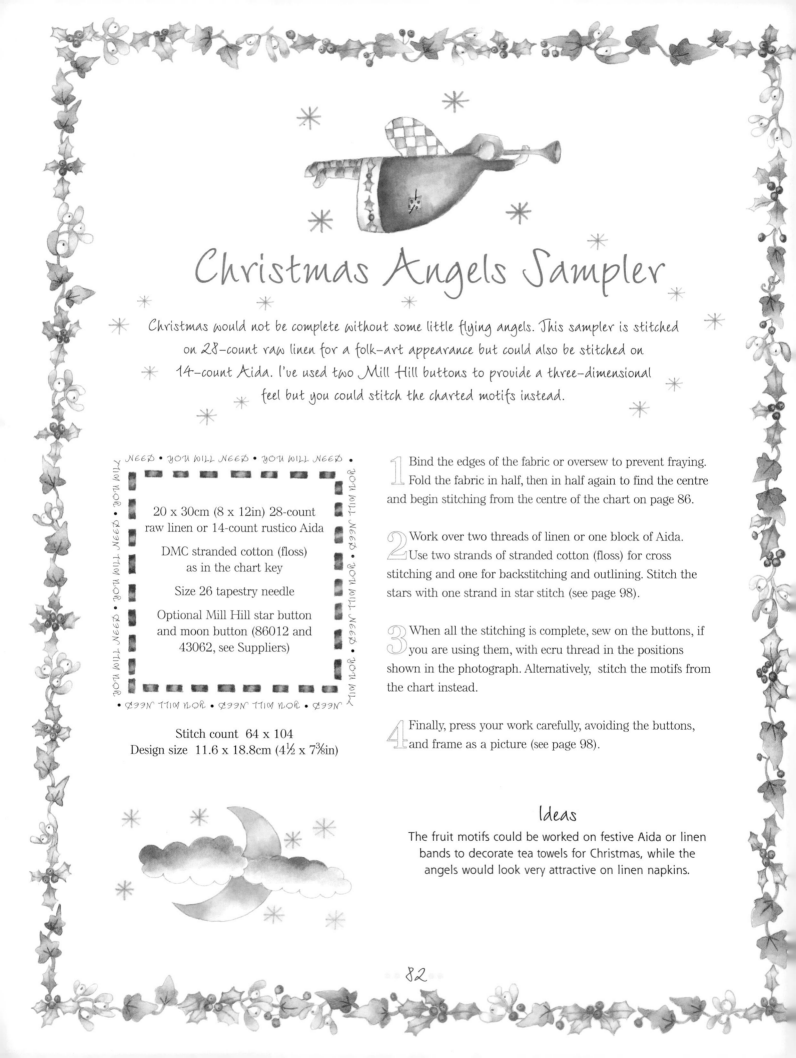

Christmas Angels Sampler

Christmas would not be complete without some little flying angels. This sampler is stitched on 28-count raw linen for a folk-art appearance but could also be stitched on 14-count Aida. I've used two Mill Hill buttons to provide a three-dimensional feel but you could stitch the charted motifs instead.

NEED • YOU WILL NEED • YOU WILL NEED

20 x 30cm (8 x 12in) 28-count raw linen or 14-count rustico Aida

DMC stranded cotton (floss) as in the chart key

Size 26 tapestry needle

Optional Mill Hill star button and moon button (86012 and 43062, see Suppliers)

Stitch count 64 x 104
Design size 11.6 x 18.8cm (4½ x 7⅜in)

1 Bind the edges of the fabric or oversew to prevent fraying. Fold the fabric in half, then in half again to find the centre and begin stitching from the centre of the chart on page 86.

2 Work over two threads of linen or one block of Aida. Use two strands of stranded cotton (floss) for cross stitching and one for backstitching and outlining. Stitch the stars with one strand in star stitch (see page 98).

3 When all the stitching is complete, sew on the buttons, if you are using them, with ecru thread in the positions shown in the photograph. Alternatively, stitch the motifs from the chart instead.

4 Finally, press your work carefully, avoiding the buttons, and frame as a picture (see page 98).

Ideas
The fruit motifs could be worked on festive Aida or linen bands to decorate tea towels for Christmas, while the angels would look very attractive on linen napkins.

Angels Bell Pull

This richly coloured design of flying angels makes a wonderful little bell pull, perfect to accompany the Christmas angels picture on the previous page. It could also be framed as a festive picture or the individual angels stitched up for cards or tree ornaments.

YOU WILL NEED

23 x 18cm (9 x 7in) cream 28-count linen or 14-count Aida

DMC stranded cotton (floss) as in the chart key

Size 26 tapestry needle

Wire hanger or bell-pull ends (The American Way, see Suppliers)

Stitch count 78 x 46
Design size 14 x 8.3cm (5½ x 3¼in)

1 Bind the edges of the fabric or oversew to prevent fraying. Fold the fabric in half, then in half again to find the centre and begin stitching from the centre of the chart on page 87.

2 Work over two threads of linen or one block of Aida. Use two strands of stranded cotton (floss) for cross stitching and one for backstitching and outlining. Stitch the stars with one strand in star stitch (see page 98).

3 When all the stitching is complete, trim the edges of the fabric and hem around the top and sides. Machine stitch a line across the bottom of the embroidery, about six rows up, and then fray the fabric up to the line. Fold the top of the hanging over the wire hanger and secure in place with slipstitching, hanging loops or a strip of Velcro.

Idea
The angels would make three charming Christmas pictures, framed in festive colours of gold, red or dark green.

Christmas Angels Sampler

DMC stranded cotton
Cross stitch

■ 310	■ 501
◪ 315	■ 3721
■ 434	■ 3776
▣ 500	▫ ecru

Backstitch and star stitch

— 310
— 434
— 3776

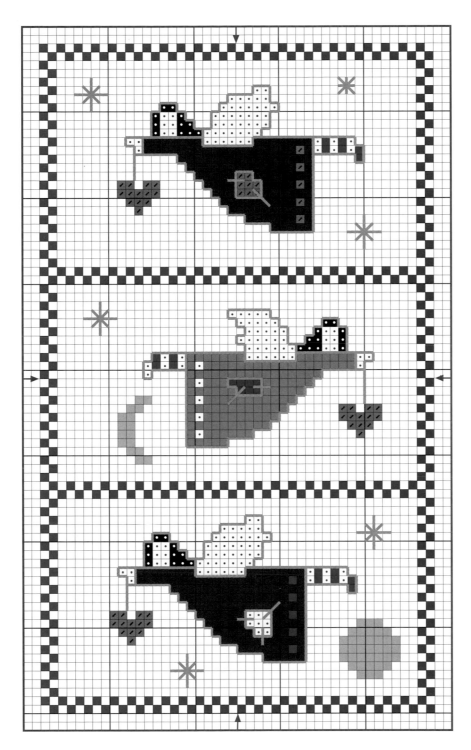

Angels Bell Pull

DMC stranded cotton
Cross stitch

■	221
▨	223
⊡	310
▧	436
■	561
◪	720
⊡	ecru

Backstitch and
star stitch

— 310

Inspirational Sampler

The idea of a fresh and pretty sampler full of good wishes and hopes to start the New Year really appealed to me. It would make a wonderful gift for a loved one, or a great project to stitch for your home. The words for this sampler were derived from an old Irish blessing and express peace and hope in every line.

38 x 33cm (15 x 13in) antique white 28-count linen or 14-count Aida

DMC stranded cotton (floss) as in the chart key

Size 26 tapestry needle

Optional Mill Hill buttons: peach posy, lemon posy and white heart (codes 86388, 86389 and 86005, see Suppliers)

Stitch count 154 x 134
Design size 28 x 24.3cm (11 x 9½in)

1 Bind the edges of the fabric or oversew to prevent fraying. Fold the fabric in half, then in half again to find the centre and begin stitching from the centre of the chart overleaf.

2 Use two strands of stranded cotton (floss) for cross stitching and one for the backstitching and outlining. Stitch over two threads of linen or one block of Aida.

3 When all the stitching is complete sew on the buttons, if you are using them, with pale pink or matching thread (see photograph for positions). Press your work carefully, avoiding the buttons, and frame as a picture (see page 98).

Idea

I have added three pastel buttons but you could use your own choice of buttons or charms – there are so many to choose from today.

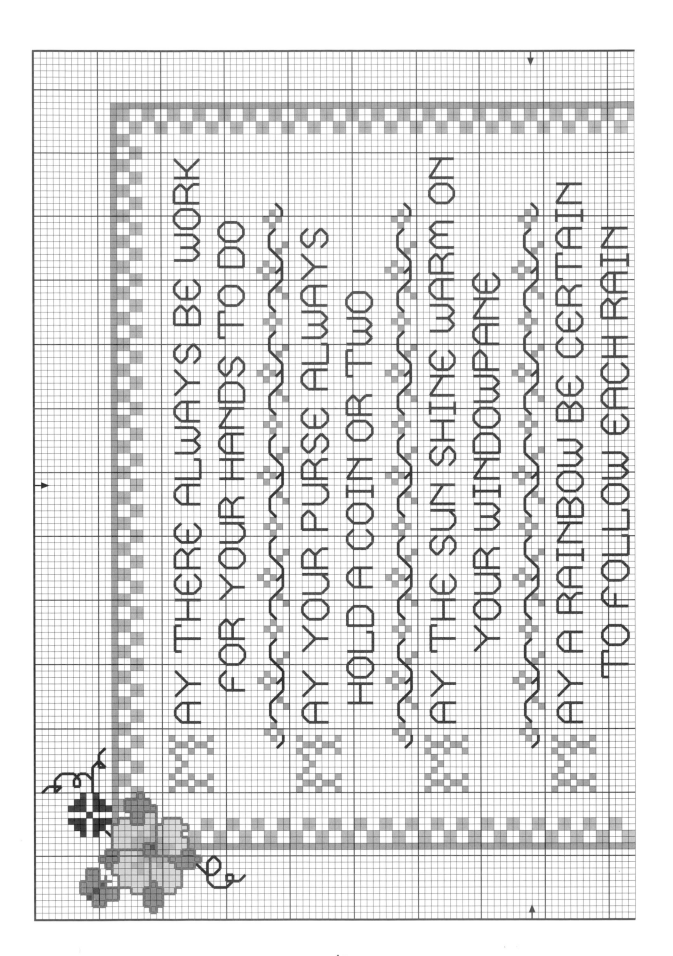

AY THERE ALWAYS BE WORK
FOR YOUR HANDS TO DO

AY YOUR PURSE ALWAYS
HOLD A COIN OR TWO

AY THE SUN SHINE WARM ON
YOUR WINDOWPANE

AY A RAINBOW BE CERTAIN
TO FOLLOW EACH RAIN

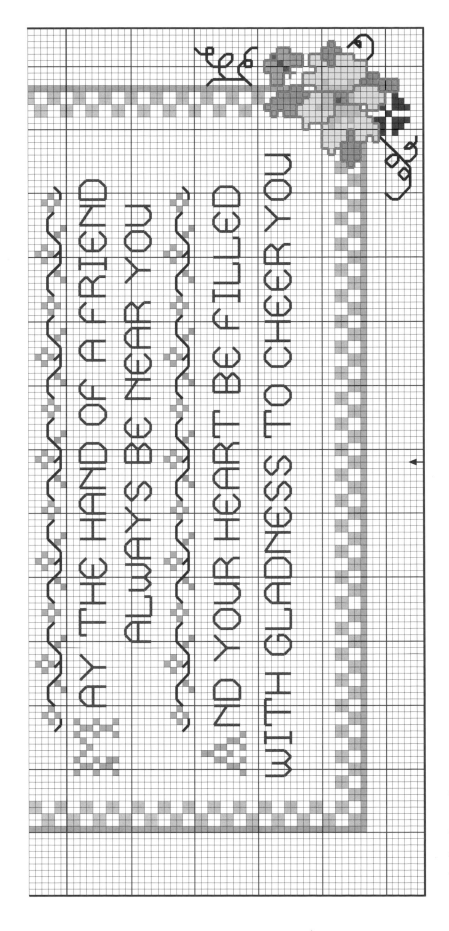

Inspirational Sampler

DMC stranded cotton
Cross stitch

■ 317	■ 703
■ 437	■ 911
■ 519	
■ 3608	■ 3822

Backstitch
— 317
— 911
— 3803

Winter Greetings Cards

This winter collection of cards offers a variety of festive ideas for you to stitch.

No Christmas would be complete without a Christmas tree card and this one is quick and easy to stitch. Adding metallic threads would bring an extra sparkle to the design.

Stitch count
43 x 42
Design size
7.8 x 7.6cm
(3¹⁄₁₆ x 3in)

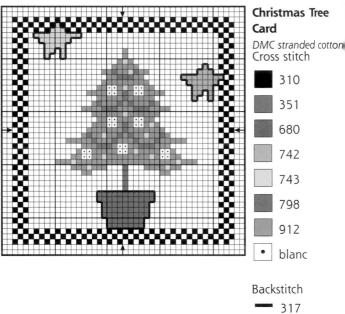

Christmas Tree Card

DMC stranded cotton
Cross stitch

■	310
■	351
■	680
■	742
■	743
■	798
■	912
•	blanc

Backstitch
— 317

A sweet little flying angel brings Christmas wishes in this card. Stitch the heart charted or use a heart charm. You could vary the design and use up odds and ends of thread to make other angels.

Stitch count
26 x 32
Design size
4.7 x 5.8cm
(1⁷⁄₈ x 2¹⁄₄in)

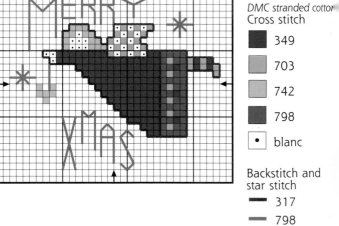

Flying Angel Card

DMC stranded cotton
Cross stitch

■	349
■	703
■	742
■	798
•	blanc

Backstitch and star stitch
— 317
— 798

Stitching Notes: Work the designs on white 14-count Aida (except the snowman which is on natural Aida and the snowy cottage which is on black) with two strands of stranded cotton (floss) for cross stitch and one for backstitch. See page 99 for making up cards and page 100 for a selection of charted messages.

Snowman Card

DMC stranded cotton
Cross stitch

- ■ 310
- ■ 349
- ■ 798
- · blanc

Backstitch
— 310

French knots
● 310

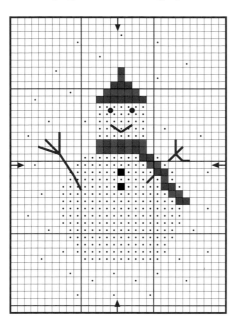

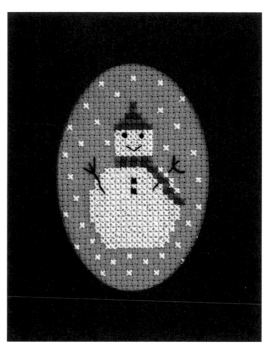

This cheery little snowman card is perfect for sending greetings at Christmas time. You could add your own message in cross stitch or backstitch.

Stitch count
37 x 26
Design size
6.7 x 4.7cm
(2⅝ x 1⅞in)

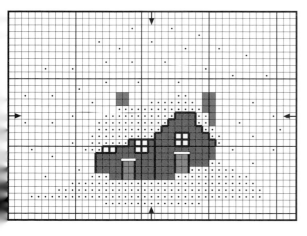

A 1920s Christmas card was the inspiration for this snowy cottage design. I love the effect of the snowflakes whirling against the night sky.

Stitch count
27 x 39
Design size
5 x 7cm
(2 x 2¾in)

Snowy Cottage Card

DMC stranded cotton
Cross stitch

- ■ 351
- ■ 913
- □ 726
- · blanc
- ■ 841

Backstitch
— 310
▭ blanc

This red heart card is perfect for sending to a loved one. The design is filled with a merry message, hearts and Christmas puddings too.

Stitch count
37 x 42
Design size
6.7 x 7.6cm
(2⅝ x 3in)

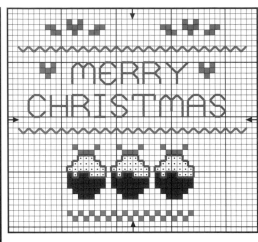

Christmas Pudding Card

DMC stranded cotton
Cross stitch

▦	161
▦	433
▦	911
▦	3328
•	blanc

Backstitch
— 317
— 500
— 3328

The bright poinsettia card is very quick to stitch. It uses a bright blue button for the vase but you could stitch the motif instead if you prefer.

Stitch count
39 x 26
Design size
7 x 4.7cm
(2¾ x 1⅞in)

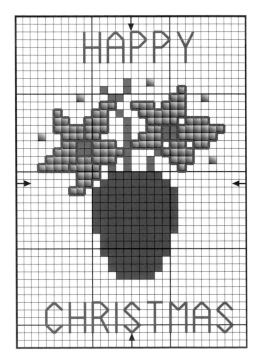

Poinsettia Card

DMC stranded cotton
Cross stitch

▦	726
▦	798
▦	911
▦	57 variegated

Backstitch
— 317
— 798

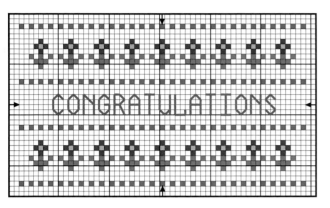

This congratulations card and the good luck card, below, are very quick to stitch and ideal to send at any time of the year.

Stitch count
32 x 57
Design size
5.8 x 10.3cm
(2$\frac{1}{4}$ x 4in)

Congratulations Card

DMC stranded cotton
Cross stitch

■ 333	■ 911	Backstitch
■ 349	■ 3827	— 500

Good Luck Card

DMC stranded cotton
Cross stitch

■ 910

/ 911

■ 913

■ 3827

Backstitch
— 500

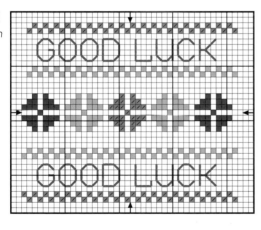

Stitch count
33 x 40
Design size
6 x 7.3cm
(2$\frac{3}{8}$ x 2$\frac{7}{8}$in)

Basic Techniques

This section contains the basic techniques you will need to work any of the projects in the book and should be particularly useful to beginners.

Preparing the Fabric

It is a good idea before starting to stitch to check the finished design size given with each project and make sure that the piece of embroidery fabric you plan to use is larger than this size. To allow for working and making up, your fabric should be at least 5–10cm (2–4in) larger all the way round than the finished size of the stitching. It is also a good idea to iron your fabric before you begin to remove any creases and then neaten and protect the edges, especially linen which frays easily, either by hemming, zigzag stitching or using masking tape which can be removed later.

Finding the centre of the fabric is necessary in order that the finished stitched design will be centred on the fabric. If you work from the centre of the chart and the centre of the fabric you cannot inadvertently work the design off the edges.

To find the centre of the fabric, fold it in half horizontally and then vertically. The centre point is where the two lines meet. You can mark the centre with a fabric marker or mark the folds with tailor's chalk or with tacked (basted) lines. As you work, this point on the fabric should correspond to the centre point on the chart. Remove any marks or tacking (basting) lines on completion of the embroidery.

Using the Charts and Keys

Each square on the chart represents one stitch. Each coloured square or square with a symbol, represents a thread colour, with the code number given in the key. This book uses DMC stranded cotton (floss) but the table on page 103 gives Anchor equivalents if required.

Some of the designs use fractional stitches (three-quarter cross stitches) to give more detail to the design or to produce the illusion of curves. These are shown on the charts by a triangle within a grid square. Solid coloured lines show where backstitches or star stitches are to be worked. French knots are shown by coloured circles. Larger coloured circles with a dot indicate beads.

Each complete chart has arrows at the sides to indicate the centre and you could mark this point with a pen or pencil. For your own use, you could enlarge the charts by colour photocopier.

Working the Stitches

The stitches used in the projects are described here, with simple diagrams.

Starting and Finishing

It is always a good idea to start and finish work neatly, avoiding bumps and threads trailing across the back of work.

To start off a length of thread using a waste knot, knot one end and push the needle through to the back of the fabric, about 2.5cm (1in) from your intended starting point, leaving the knot on the right side (see Fig 1). Stitch towards the knot, securing the thread at the back of the fabric as you go. When the thread is secure, cut off the knot.

To begin stitching with a loop start, use one strand of thread doubled, threading the needle with the two ends. Put the needle through the fabric from the wrong side, leaving a loop at the back (see Fig 2). Form a half cross stitch, put the needle back through the fabric and through the loop to anchor the stitch.

To finish off a thread or start a new thread, weave the needle and thread into the back of several worked stitches and then trim off neatly.

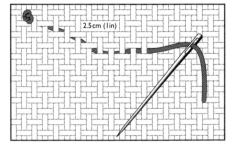

Fig 1 Away waste knot start

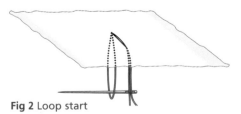

Fig 2 Loop start

Backstitching and Outlining

Backstitch is indicated on the charts by a solid coloured line. It can be worked on its own for lettering, on top of other stitches for detail and as an outline around areas of completed cross stitches to add definition. Most backstitch is worked with one strand of thread – check the project instructions.

To work backstitch follow Fig 3, bringing the needle up through the fabric at 1 and down at 2. Bring it back up at 3 and then down at 1. Repeat the process to make the next stitch. This produces short stitches on the front of the work and longer ones on the back.

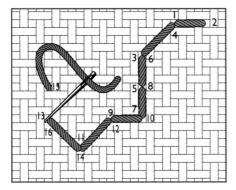

Fig 3 Backstitch

Cross Stitch

This is the main stitch used throughout the projects and each complete cross stitch is represented on the charts by a coloured square. The cross stitches in this book are worked over one block of Aida fabric or over two threads of linen.

A single cross stitch on Aida is worked in two stages: a diagonal stitch is worked over one block and then a second diagonal is worked over the first stitch in the opposite direction, forming a cross (see Fig 4). The same principle applies if working on an evenweave such as linen, except the stitch is worked over two fabric threads (see Fig 5).

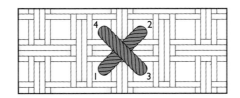

Fig 4 A single cross stitch on Aida

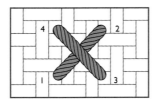

Fig 5 A single cross stitch on linen

If you have a large area to cover, you may prefer to work the cross stitches in rows. If working on Aida, follow Fig 6, stitching a row of half cross stitches in one direction, and then working back in the opposite direction with the diagonal stitches needed to complete each cross stitch. The upper stitches of all the crosses should lie in the same direction to produce a neat effect. Fig 7 shows cross stitch in rows worked on evenweave.

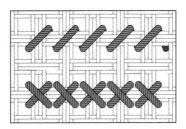

Fig 6 Cross stitches in rows on Aida

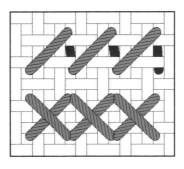

Fig 7 Cross stitches in rows on linen

French Knot

This useful little stitch is used in addition to cross stitch to add texture, emphasis and highlights. In this book French knots are usually work with one or two strands of thread and are shown on the charts by a small coloured circle.

To work a French knot, bring the needle up to the right side of the fabric, hold the thread down with your left thumb (if right-handed) and wind the thread around the needle twice. Still holding the thread taut, put the needle through to the back of the work, one thread or part of a block away from the entry point (see Fig 8a and b). If you want bigger knots, add more thread to the needle.

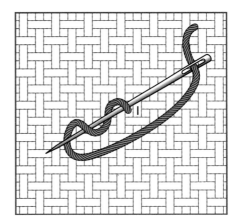

Fig 8a Working a French knot

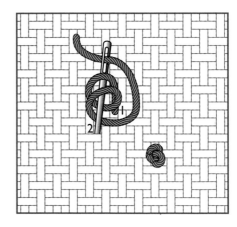

Fig 8b

Star Stitch

This stitch has been worked on some of the samplers and cards to create simple stars. Follow Fig 9, working in the same direction around each stitch, passing the needle down through the central hole. You can vary the length and number of 'arms' to create different star shapes (Fig 10).

Fig 9 Working star stitch

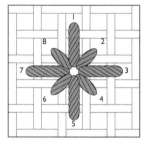

Fig 10 A star stitch variation

Three-quarter Cross Stitch

This is a part or fractional stitch. Work a half cross stitch, then add a quarter stitch in the opposite direction, bringing the needle down in the centre of the half cross stitch already worked (see Fig 11).

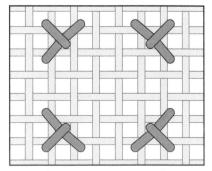

Fig 11 Three-quarter cross stitch

Working with Beads, Buttons and Charms

Many of the samplers in the book feature pretty beads, buttons and charms. Adding beads can bring interesting sparkle and texture to a cross stitch design, while buttons and charms can echo the cross stitch theme and provide focal points.

Beads, especially seed beads, are best sewn in place with a half or whole cross stitch (see Fig 12), using thread which matches the fabric colour and a beading needle or a very fine 'sharp' needle.

The positions of the buttons and charms used in the designs are clearly shown on the photographs but you may prefer to attach them in a different place, or use other buttons you have found. Stitch securely into position with thread that matches the button or fabric.

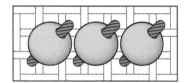

Fig 12 Attaching beads

Caring for Finished Work

Cross stitch embroidery can be washed and ironed, though care should be taken if the work has delicate ceramic buttons. Make sure it is colourfast first, then wash with bleach-free soap in hand-hot water, squeezing gently but never rubbing or wringing. Rinse in plenty of cold or lukewarm water and dry naturally.

To iron cross stitch embroidery, use a hot setting on a steam iron. Cover the ironing board with a thick layer of towelling and place the stitching on this, right side down. Press the fabric firmly but avoid any charms, buttons or metallic threads used.

Mounting and Framing Embroidery

It really is best to take large samplers and pictures to a professional framer, where you will be able to choose from a wide variety of mounts and frames that will best enhance your work. The framer will be able to lace and stretch the fabric correctly and cut any surrounding mounts accurately, including unusual shapes such as hearts.

If mounting work into commercial products, such as box lids, follow the manufacturer's instructions. For small pieces of work, back with lightweight iron-on interfacing to prevent the fabric wrinkling, and then mount.

If you intend to mount the work yourself, use acid-free mounting board in a colour that will not show through the embroidery. Cut the mount board to fit inside your picture frame and allow for the thickness of the fabric pulled over the edges of the board. There are two common methods used for securing an embroidery to a piece of mount board – taping and lacing.

Taping Method

Place the cut board on the back of the embroidery in the position required. Starting from the centre of one of the longest edges, fold the fabric over the board and pin through the fabric into the edge of the board to keep the fabric from moving. Check it is in the correct place with no wrinkles or bumps, then stick the work in place using strips of double-sided adhesive tape, removing the pins once finished (see Fig 13).

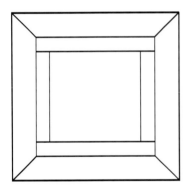

Fig 13 Mounting work by taping

Lacing Method

Pin the work in place on the board, as described above, then working from the centre and using long lengths of very strong thread, lace backwards and forwards across the gap (see Fig 14). Repeat this process for the shorter sides, taking care to mitre or fold the corners in neatly. Remove the pins once finished.

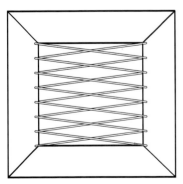

Fig 14 Mounting work by lacing

Mounting Work into Cards

There are many lovely card mounts available today in craft and needlework shops and through mail-order companies and needlecraft magazines. They usually come pre-folded with three sections, the middle one having a window for your embroidery. Choose a card design that complements your embroidery, making sure that the window is large enough to house your design.

You could also make your own greetings cards using some of the lovely handmade papers and cards available today. These can be further embellished with beads, buttons, ribbons, bows, metallic cord or raffia. Using stamps, stencils and calligraphy pens can also add a personal touch to your card designs.

To mount your finished embroidery in a card, first make sure your embroidery looks good in the window space, then trim your design to the correct size to fit. Position small lengths of double-sided adhesive tape around the window area (see Fig 15). Remove the backing

from the tape and lay the card on top of the embroidery so that it shows neatly through the window. Press into place. Fold over the third of the card that covers the back of the embroidery, ensuring that the card opens correctly before securing with more double-sided tape.

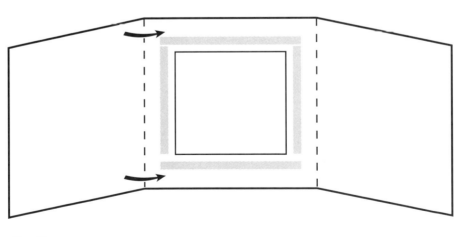

Fig 15

Alternative Messages

Use these messages to customize the designs in the book – they will be particularly useful for cards. Use graph paper to plan your message before you begin to stitch, using the colours suggested in the charts or your own choice.

Alphabets and Numerals

These letters and numbers can be used to personalize samplers and cards. Plan names, dates and messages on graph paper before you begin to stitch to ensure the words will fit the space available. Use the colours suggested in the charts or choose your own.

The designs in this book use DMC stranded cottons (floss) but Anchor equivalents are given here. This thread conversion table is only a guide, as exact colour comparisons cannot always be made. An asterisk * indicates an Anchor shade that has been used more than once so take care to avoid duplication in a design. If you wish to use Madeira threads, telephone for a conversion chart on 01845 524880 or email: acts@madeira.co.uk

DMC	Anchor	DMC	Anchor	DMC	Anchor	DMC	Anchor	DMC	Anchor	DMC	Anchor	DMC	Anchor	DMC	Anchor
B 5200	1	355	1014	604	55	781	308*	912	209	3023	899	3765	170	3846	1090
White	2	356	1013*	605	1094	782	308*	913	204	3024	388*	3766	167	3847	1076*
Ecru	387*	367	216	606	334	783	307	915	1029	3031	905*	3768	779	3848	1074*
150	59	368	214	608	330*	791	178	917	89	3032	898*	3770	1009	3849	1070*
151	73	369	1043	610	889	792	941	918	341	3033	387*	3772	1007	3850	188*
152	969	370	888*	611	898*	793	176*	919	340	3041	871	3773	1008	3851	186*
153	95*	371	887*	612	832	794	175	920	1004	3042	870	3774	778	3852	306*
154	873	372	887*	613	831	796	133	921	1003*	3045	888*	3776	1048*	3853	1003*
155	1030*	400	351	632	936	797	132	922	1003*	3046	887	3777	1015	3854	313
156	118*	402	1047*	640	393	798	146	924	851	3047	887	3778	1013*	3855	311*
157	120*	407	914	642	392	799	145	926	850	3051	845*	3779	868	3856	347
158	178	413	236*	644	391	800	144	927	849	3052	844	3781	1050	3857	936*
159	120*	414	235*	645	273	801	359	928	274	3053	843	3782	388*	3858	1007
160	175*	415	398	646	8581*	806	169	930	1035	3064	883	3787	904*	3859	914*
161	176	420	374	647	1040	807	168	931	1034	3072	397	3790	904*	3860	379*
162	159*	422	372	648	900	809	130	932	1033	3078	292	3799	236*	3861	378
163	877	433	358	666	46	813	161*	934	852*	3325	129	3801	1098	3862	358*
164	240*	434	310	676	891	814	45	935	861	3326	36	3802	1019*	3863	379*
165	278*	435	365	677	361*	815	44	936	846	3328	1024	3803	69	3864	376
166	280*	436	363	680	901*	816	43	937	268*	3340	329	3804	63*	3865	2*
167	375*	437	362	699	923*	817	13*	938	381	3341	328	3805	62*	3866	926*
168	274*	444	291	700	228	818	23*	939	152*	3345	268*	3806	62*	48	1207
169	849*	445	288	701	227	819	271	943	189	3346	267*	3807	122	51	1220*
208	110	451	233	702	226	820	134	945	881	3347	266*	3808	1068	52	1209*
209	109	452	232	703	238	822	390	946	332	3348	264	3809	1066*	57	1203*
210	108	453	231	704	256*	823	152*	947	330*	3350	77	3810	1066*	61	1218*
211	342	469	267*	712	926	824	164	948	1011	3354	74	3811	1060	62	1202*
221	897*	470	266*	718	88	825	162*	950	4146	3362	263	3812	188	67	1212
223	895	471	265	720	326	826	161*	951	1010	3363	262	3813	875*	69	1218*
224	895	472	253	721	324	827	160	954	203*	3364	261	3814	1074	75	1206*
225	1026	498	1005	722	323*	828	9159	955	203*	3371	382	3815	877*	90	1217*
300	352	500	683	725	305*	829	906	956	40*	3607	87	3816	876*	91	1211
301	1049*	501	878	726	295*	830	277*	957	50	3608	86	3817	875*	92	1215*
304	19	502	877*	727	293	831	277*	958	187	3609	85	3818	923*	93	1210*
307	289	503	876*	729	890	832	907*	959	186	3685	1028	3819	278	94	1216
309	42	504	206*	730	845*	833	874*	961	76*	3687	68	3820	306	95	1209*
310	403	517	162*	731	281*	834	874*	962	75*	3688	75*	3821	305*	99	1204
311	148	518	1039	732	281*	838	1088	963	23*	3689	49	3822	295*	101	1213*
312	979	519	1038	733	280	839	1086	964	185	3705	35*	3823	386	102	1209*
315	1019*	520	862*	734	279	840	1084	966	240	3706	33*	3824	8*	103	1210*
316	1017	522	860	738	361*	841	1082	970	925	3708	31	3825	323*	104	1217*
317	400	523	859	739	366	842	1080	971	316*	3712	1023	3826	1049*	105	1218*
318	235*	524	858	740	316*	844	1041	972	298	3713	1020	3827	311	106	1203*
319	1044*	535	401	741	304	869	375	973	290	3716	25	3828	373	107	1203*
320	215	543	933	742	303	890	218	975	357	3721	896	3829	901*	108	1220*
321	47	550	101*	743	302	891	35*	976	1001	3722	1027	3830	5975	111	1218*
322	978	552	99	744	301	892	33*	977	1002	3726	1018	3831	29	112	1201*
326	59*	553	98	745	300	893	27	986	246	3727	1016	3832	28	113	1210*
327	101*	554	95	746	275	894	26	987	244	3731	76*	3833	31*	114	1213*
333	119	561	212	747	158	895	1044*	988	243	3733	75*	3834	100*	115	1206*
334	977	562	210	754	1012	898	380	989	242	3740	872	3835	98*	121	1210*
335	40*	563	208	758	9575	899	38	991	1076	3743	869	3836	90	122	1215*
336	150	564	206*	760	1022	900	333	992	1072	3746	1030	3837	100*	124	1210*
340	118	580	924	761	1021	902	897*	993	1070	3747	120	3838	177	125	1213*
341	117*	581	281*	762	234	904	258	995	410	3750	1036	3839	176*	126	1209*
347	1025	597	1064	772	259*	905	257	996	433	3752	1032	3840	120*		
349	13*	598	1062	775	128	906	256*	3011	856	3753	1031	3841	159*		
350	11	600	59*	776	24	907	255	3012	855	3755	140	3842	164*		
351	10	601	63*	778	968	909	923*	3013	853	3756	1037	3843	1089*		
352	9	602	57	779	380*	910	230	3021	905*	3760	162*	3844	410*		
353	8*	603	62*	780	309	911	205	3022	8581*	3761	928	3845	1089*		

Suppliers

UK

The American Way
30 Edgbaston Road, Smethwick, West
Midlands B66 4LQ, UK
tel: 0121 601 5454
*For Mill Hill buttons, charms, wire
hangers and many other supplies*

Coats Crafts UK
PO Box 22, Lingfield Estate,
McMullen Road, Darlington,
County Durham DL1 1YQ, UK
tel: 01325 365457 (for a list of stockists)
*For Anchor stranded cotton (floss) and
other embroidery supplies (Coats also
supply some Charles Craft products)*

Craft Creations Limited
1C Ingersoll House, Delamare Road,
Cheshunt, Herts EN8 9HD, UK
tel: 019992 781900
website: www.craftcreations.com
*For greetings card blanks
and card-making accessories*

From Debbie Cripps
31 Lower Whitelands, Radstock,
Bath BA3 3JW, UK
website: www.debbiecripps.co.uk
*For buttons, charms
and embroidery supplies*

Dee Fine Arts
182 Telegraph Road, Heswall,
Wirral CH60 0AJ, UK
tel: 0151 3426657
For expert embroidery and picture framing

DMC Creative World
Pullman Road, Wigston,
Leicestershire LE18 2DY, UK
tel: 0116 281 1040
fax: 0116 281 3592
website: www.dmc/cw.com
*For a huge range of threads, fabrics
and needlework supplies*

Framecraft Miniatures Ltd
372–376 Summer Lane, Hockley,
Birmingham B19 3QA, UK
tel: 0121 212 0551
fax: 0121 212 0552
website: www.framecraft.com
*For Mill Hill buttons, charms
and many ready-made items*

John Lewis
(Branches in many UK towns and cities)
*For general haberdashery, ribbons, felt,
trimmings and embroidery supplies*

Voirrey Embroidery Centre
Brimstage Hall, Wirral CH63 6JA, UK
tel: 0151 342 3514
fax: 0151 342 5161
*For embroidery supplies, books
and exhibitions*

Willow Fabrics
27 Willow Green,
Knutsford WA16 6AX, UK
tel: 0156562 1098
fax: 01565 653233
*For linen, evenweave and
Aida fabrics, stitching paper
and many other supplies*

Merry Heart Designs
For cross stitch charts and books
by Helen Philipps
tel: 0151 625 1682
website: www.merryheart.co.uk

US

Charles Craft Inc
PO Box 1049, Laurenburg,
NC 28353, USA
tel: 910 844 3521
email: ccraft@carolina.net
website: www.charlescraft.com
*Cross stitch fabrics and many useful
pre-finished items*

Gay Bowles Sales Inc
PO Box 1060, Janesville,
WI 53547, USA
tel: 608 754 9466
fax: 608 754 0665
email: millhill@inwave.com
website: www.millhill.com
*For Mill Hill buttons and beads and
a US source for Framecraft products*

Zweigart/Joan Toggit Ltd
262 Old Brunswick Road,
Suite E, Piscataway,
NJ 08854-3756, USA
tel: 732 562 8888
email: info@zweigart.com
website: www.zweigart.com
*For cross stitch fabrics and
pre-finished items*

Acknowledgments

Thank you to everyone at David & Charles, especially to Cheryl Brown for commissioning this book and for her creative inspiration and encouragement; to Lin Clements for her attention to detail and superb editing of both text and charts; and to Ali Myer and Prudence Rogers for their beautiful book design. Thank you to Simon Whitmore for his wonderful photography. Thanks to Cara Ackerman at DMC Creative World for supplying me with all the gorgeous threads I need, and to The American Way for generously supplying the Mill Hill buttons. Finally, a big thank you to all my family for their love and support as always.

About the Author

Helen Philipps studied printed textiles and embroidery at Manchester Metropolitan University and then taught drawing and design before becoming a freelance designer. After working in the greetings industry, Helen's love of needlecraft led to her creating original designs for stitching magazines and her work is still featured regularly in *Cross Stitch Collection*, *Cross Stitcher* and *World of Cross Stitching*. In 2000 she set up Merry Heart Designs which specializes in bright, modern cross stitch charts. This is Helen's third book to be published by David & Charles.

Index